why Do
You care?
fal

I came to think —
Th...
Co...
T...

Who was God's grace w/ skin on for You?

TOUCH
Pressing Against the Wounds of a Broken World

RUDY RASMUS

FOREWORD BY DR. KIRBYJON CALDWELL

P. 88
P. 104 — Cold Sunday — P. 128
P. 117 *

THOMAS NELSON
Since 1798

NASHVILLE DALLAS MEXICO CITY RIO DE JANEIRO BEIJING

Published in Nashville, Tennessee, by Thomas Nelson. Thomas Nelson is a registered trademark of Thomas Nelson, Inc.

Thomas Nelson, Inc., titles may be purchased in bulk for educational, business, fund-raising, or sales promotional use. For information, please e-mail SpecialMarkets@thomasnelson.com.

This book uses both the New King James Version and the New International Version of the Bible.

Scripture taken from the New King James Version. © 1982 by Thomas Nelson, Inc. Used by permission. All rights reserved.

Scripture taken from the HOLY BIBLE, NEW INTERNATIONAL VERSION®. © 1973, 1978, 1984 International Bible Society. Used by permission of Zondervan. All rights reserved.

The "NIV" and "New International Version" trademarks are registered in the United States Patent and Trademark Office by International Bible Society. Use of either trademark requires the permission of International Bible Society.

Managing Editor: Adria Haley
Cover design: Will Stacy IV of Garage Door Media
Page design: Mandi Cofer

Library of Congress Cataloging-in-Publication data on file with the Library of Congress.

ISBN 978-0-8499-1985-5

Printed in the United States of America

08 09 10 11 RRD 7 6 5 4 3 2

This book is dedicated to my father, Rudolph Valentino Rasmus (1928–2004), who always affectionately called me "Mr. President," "Boss Man," or "Big Shot." My dad had a perceptive understanding of people, a crazy sense of humor, a veiled but enormous capacity for compassion, and an ability to curse poetically with anyone in any setting. His example equipped me for life. I miss him, and I will always appreciate his impact on me. On July 4, 2004, Dad experienced his own personal Independence Day!

I also dedicate this book to my mom, Mildred Thomas Rasmus, whose well-timed, hard left hook and consistent support not only kept me from completely losing my mind during my younger years, but provided the framework for care and concern that shaped my ministry.

CONTENTS

ACKNOWLEDGMENTS

How can I thank everyone who has helped and supported in the awesome task of writing this book? To all of you, I want to say, *Thank you!*

I have been blessed with many amazing people who shared their lives with me over the years. They are so numerous that I'm afraid I'd leave someone out if I tried to name them all. To all of you, I say again, *Thank you!* I deeply appreciate your thoughtfulness, support, care, prayers and sacrifice throughout the years. Without you, none of what we have experienced could have happened.

In a category of her own, I want to thank my wife, Juanita, who reintroduced me to love, to life, and to Christ. As Jackie Wilson's song says, "Your love lifted me higher than I've ever been lifted before." You are something else! When we met at that funeral twenty-one years ago, I knew I had met the person God had sent me to love forever. You have skydived, hiked two mountains, and trekked around the world, and you are just getting started. Thank you for being you. *I love you.*

To my daughters, Morgan and Ryan, my life was completed when you were born. Both of you are my hope for the future. I am so proud of you. From the time you were little girls, you have been my teachers by showing me the importance of fun, freedom, and fantasy in life. *I love you both.*

I am deeply grateful for my dear friend and brother, Pastor Kirbyjon Caldwell. Throughout our twenty-year friendship, I have been constantly amazed by your ability to see possibilities in impossible people, and to trust in things unseen with the expectation of tangible results. Thank you for an incredible seminary education over the breakfast table and by telephone in those early years. And thank you for giving me the opportunity to serve God at St. John's. I am in ministry today because of your willingness to mentor me, and you trusted me to go it alone. *Thank you.*

Jonathan Gregory, thanks for driving the freight train beginning in 1992. Christian Washington, thank you for pushing me to get the book done. Joe Daniels, Dred Scott, Andre Johnson, and Vance Ross, thank you for praying me through this process. Pat Springle, thank you for generously sharing your publishing expertise and pushing me even more to get this done.

To the staff of the Bread of Life, Inc., The St. John's Academy, and St. John's Downtown: I am blessed to be a part of your lives, and equally blessed to have had the opportunity to work alongside each of you. *Thank you.*

The early pioneers (you know who you are) and many others prayed and worked tirelessly to advance God's work in our community. *Thank you for hanging in there.*

The members of St. John's have sacrificed and labored to make our church a great faith community. Your incredible capacity to love God and other people is amazing, and your constancy, allegiance, and support are wonderful. Even more amazing is your unswerving commitment to accept everyone unconditionally. You have steadfastly made St. John's into a lighthouse instead of a yacht club, and you have faithfully affirmed St. John's as an emergency room instead of a waiting room. You have loyally faced challenge after challenge on behalf of the least and the last in our world.

And to everyone, always remember: *"I love you, and there's nothing you can do about it!"*

FOREWORD

What God has accomplished through Rudy Rasmus in downtown Houston is nothing short of a miracle. Only by God's grace and God's empowerment could a failing, inner-city church be transformed into a thriving megachurch. Rudy sees with God's vision: he saw assets where others only saw deficits, and he brings hope to the hopeless. The principles of his ministry are based on the simple but powerful premise that God's love radically changes lives. The ministry of St. John's exposes fear, hurt, and doubt in each of us, and it lavishes love to heal these wounds. This is precisely the way Jesus treated people, and it's the way Jesus calls us today to touch the lives of every person in our communities, from the fabulously wealthy to "the least of these."

I remember the first time I saw Rudy. He was sitting in the congregation at Windsor Village, and he looked like he was analyzing everything. Soon after that day, we talked. He told me one of his business interests was, quite frankly, unique, but his presence at church told me he was genuinely interested in pursuing Christ. Rudy joined a men's Bible study, and he became involved in several ministries of the church.

As I got to know Rudy, I sensed I could trust him. I soon learned he is an astute businessman. Our church has always pursued entrepreneurial economic development opportunities, so I asked Rudy for advice in the church's real estate ventures. We developed a genuine friendship.

When the denomination asked Windsor Village to take over the facility at St. John's, I asked Rudy to look at the property. From the viewpoint of every other denominational executive, it wasn't a great location for anything. That's why Rudy's report surprised me. He told me it was "a great location." He believed St. John's was perfectly positioned for an outreach to the entire community: the wealthy, the middle class, and the homeless. I was impressed with his vision, and even more impressed when Rudy told me that God was calling him to coordinate the ministry at St. John's.

Since Rudy took over the faltering ministry at St. John's downtown, God has used him to build a ministry far beyond anything anyone could have expected. Rudy's personality and God-given gifts fit St. John's like a glove. He is as comfortable meeting with city council members as he is with indigent addicts. He is a remarkable man—and a remarkable leader. Beginning with very few resources and ministering to people in an urban community, God has used Rudy to build a phenomenal ministry where people experience the love, compassion, and strength of God.

Though Rudy has experienced incredible success, he is still the same man who thirsts for God and stays connected to people from every walk of life. His authentic love for every person who walks through the doors of St. John's tells me all I need to know about Rudy Rasmus. I'm proud to call him my friend.

Dr. Kirbyjon Caldwell
Windsor Village United Methodist Church, Houston, Texas

PART 1
A Touch That Transforms Lives

CHAPTER 1
Sometimes, It's Messy

*Then Jesus, moved with compassion, stretched out His
hand and touched him, and said to him, "I am willing;
be cleansed"* (MARK 1:41 NKJV).

*Whatever makes us feel superior to other people, whatever
tempts us to convey a sense of superiority, that is the gravity of
our sinful nature, not grace.* —PHILLIP YANCEY

He came barreling down the aisle—police in hot pursuit—
cradling something shiny under his arm and sweating heavily in
jeans, no shirt, no shoes . . . wild-eyed and dangerous looking for
such a young, skinny man. The guest preacher looked over at me
and kept preaching. He was the U.S. ambassador to Tanzania, had
traveled extensively, and had vast experience in unique situations.
He'd survived the bombing of Tanzania's embassy; we both knew he
could handle a little interruption in an eight o'clock church service.

Truth is, despite the big stained-glass windows, vaulted ceiling,
and theaterlike stage that clearly indicate "church," we have little

3

interruptions like this about once a quarter at St. John's. Sometimes it's threatening, sometimes comical, sometimes insane, but every "interrupter" looking for sanctuary . . . a spiritual shelter. We serve a part of downtown Houston that attracts every segment of society from 150 zip codes—a melting pot of wealthy and powerful, poor and fragile, educated and uneducated, very young and very old, black, white, and brown. For ninety minutes every Sunday, the lines of class distinction disappear and the pews are packed with white-collar professionals, the family next door, the homeless and addicts. And I was looking at an addict.

The wild man jumped on the stage, turned and faced the congregation—the more conservative, traditional, and less reactionary crowd of the day. If this was happening in the ten o'clock service, we'd need the police to pull the crowd off this intruder. I moved from the stage to the front row to get his attention. *What is under his arm*, I wondered. *Is it a gun?* I knew the two policemen—armed and in full uniform—were wondering the same thing. Neither had drawn his weapon, but the moment was tense. They hung back as instructed, waiting for my signal, unwilling to make a bigger scene until absolutely necessary. The preacher kept preaching without pause. The young man looked around frantically, curly afro bobbing, breathing hard, but in just moments we made eye contact. I smiled at him, and he smiled back—a big, toothy smile that transformed him from a threat to a need. *There's a happy child in there,* I thought and motioned to him. "Come on over and sit next to me."

He came over and sat down. The police watched and waited—just like everybody else in the service. I leaned over and asked him, "Man, what are you running from?" His big eyes looked at me in horror, and he said, "Hell." And then I did something I challenge the congregants to do every Sunday—namely, look your neighbors in the eye, then exchange greetings and hugs. I put my arm around his slight frame; he relaxed, and a CD case slipped from under his arm. No gun . . . no weapon. Someone brought him a shirt from the back. The preacher called the young man to the stage and prayed for him, and God did something amazing right then—God gave His calming, healing touch. The fear and phobia were gone. The preacher wrapped up his sermon, and I began talking to this young man.

His name was Patrick, he was twenty-five years old, and he'd just escaped from the county psychiatric hospital by jumping the fence. He'd been placed there a day earlier for having a psychotic episode. He'd been smoking marijuana laced with formaldehyde, street name "wet," and he'd been hallucinating. "Wet" is a particularly wicked drug—it opens the user's spirit and brain to terrifying demonic encounters that have a paranoid-schizophrenic appearance. Patrick confirmed he'd had a firsthand encounter with the devil. But while locked up, he remembered hearing St. John's would be a safe place for him. He ran here as fast as he could. He wasn't carrying a gun; he was carrying hope.

And that's what St. John's is all about: a sanctuary, a place of safety and freedom for hurting people to be who they are authentically—whether crazed or sick or sad or lonely or desperate or just in need of loving human touch and a little hope. Sure, this creates some high drama at times. We hire off-duty cops for our congregants' safety. We get interrupted. Members get irritated and ask me when I'm going to "do something about all these . . . *people*." I tell members what I won't do: I won't push these people aside or make them sit in the back or parade them to the front row to make a spectacle of them. What I will *do* is love them unconditionally, and treat them with grace and dignity.

Congregants at St. John's understand what it is to be poor, to have broken relationships, to lose a loved one to death. We have a common denominator of understanding human suffering. So we might be the only chance for people like Patrick . . . people on their own drug-marked odysseys, looking for that warmth and acceptance missing in society. We are missionaries; we simply pose as a church.

The wild young man committed that Sunday to turn his life around. And he has. He started attending services and has a wife and two kids coming with him. Six St. John's men have agreed to call Patrick every week, and his life is starting to take a turn. His recovery has not been perfect, but he desperately wants his life to permanently change. And that's all we—and the Lord—require.

That was the eight o'clock service. When the ten o'clock service began, Patrick was walking out of the church as his father came walking in. They were estranged and hadn't seen each other in a long time. They hugged joyously and sat together for the second service. It was his father's first visit to St. John's, and I guess he was desperate for some hope, too. It was a beautiful thing to see.

OLD LESSONS . . . AND NEW

"Never trust preachers and church folk."

That was one of the lessons my dad taught me, and I believed him. My only contact with religious people revealed their poisonous blend of self-righteousness and hypocrisy. I didn't mind making money off them, but I sure wasn't attracted to them in any way. Things, though, were about to change.

After Juanita and I had been married for a few years and the girls were very young, I decided I'd go with them to church. I wasn't going because I had some kind of experience with God. Only went because it was the right thing to do. I didn't hate it, but it sure didn't cause any fireworks, either.

Months later, I decided to join a men's group, and suddenly, I was opening the Bible and reading the gospel accounts of Jesus' life. I was fascinated by how He related to men and women—people on the edge—people just like me. He didn't care who people were. He just loved them. And His love wasn't some pious statement uttered from a distance; He touched them! He intentionally reached out and touched poor people, sick people, unclean people, society's outcasts, precocious children, and anybody else who wanted to connect with Him.

STILL TOUCHING PEOPLE . . . LIKE ME

As I read story after story of Jesus' interaction with people, I realized that He's the same today as He was then . . . He's just invisible now. He still wants to touch people, and He was touching me at that very moment. I was desperate and empty. My life was headed in the wrong direction, and I knew it. I opened my heart to Jesus and began the most life-changing relationship ever known to man. He touched me just as He touched the leper, the blind man, the crippled guy, the kids, and the dead girl. They were all forgiven and given new life. So was I!

As the weeks went by, God melted my calloused heart. I had been guarded, but now His love allowed me to be open. I had been tough, but He replaced my defensiveness with compassion and kindness. I had been angry, but now His forgiveness assured me I was cleansed. I had depended on my own abilities, but He showed me that I could trust in His power to accomplish far greater purposes than I'd ever dreamed. The more I experienced the touch of His love, kindness, forgiveness, and strength, the more revolution God caused in my

I realized that it wasn't just a good thing to reach out to the marginalized—I had to defend their right to be here.

heart. I began to see myself as an advocate for the marginalized around me: drug addicts, homeless people, gays and lesbians, gang members, and misfits—people I had never cared for before.

Nobody at the church put up roadblocks for a new believer who wanted to help outcasts in our community, so not long after I trusted in Jesus as my Savior, I found myself neck deep in ministry to those people. After a couple of years (I'll tell more of that story later), my friend and mentor, Kirbyjon Caldwell, asked me to take leadership of a dying church in Houston's inner city. Soon, homeless people and addicts sat in the pews with people of power and prominence. It was thrilling! It looked like the kingdom of God to me, but the kingdom came at a cost. One day, a well-dressed lady who was a corporate professional came to me with a complaint. "Rudy," she said with a tone of disgust, "things just don't seem to be improving around here. What are you going to do about all of *those people?*"

I knew exactly who she was referring to. She was the spokesperson for some upwardly mobile professionals who were dissatisfied with our church. At that moment, God gave me a clear insight, and I made a choice: From that moment, I realized that it wasn't just *a good thing* to reach out to the marginalized—I had to *defend their right* to be here. She had meant her comment to correct my wayward thinking, but I took it as a clear signal from God to champion the people she despised.

That's what Jesus did when He walked among us.

In Jesus' world, people who felt superior to the sick, blind, lame, and demon-possessed often went to Jesus with their complaints. It's the same today. Like the lady who looked down her nose at "those people," they feel completely righteous when they ask questions such as, "Pastor Rudy, what are we going to do with all these gays and lesbians [or addicts or mentally ill or gang members or homeless people or whoever] who come to church here?" or "Can you help us figure out what to do about that person's smell?" or "Pastor, can you help me? I just don't feel safe around people like that."

When I hear questions like these, I ask, "Who are the people you're talking about? What are their names? Tell me about their lives. How many *people* are we talking about?" And in the vast majority of cases, I receive only blank stares in reply. The inquisitors have made a value judgment based on outward appearance. They haven't taken the time to know these people, to touch their lives in meaningful ways. Their prejudice is based on ignorance of the real person. But Jesus had given me a love for all these people, so I was unwilling to tolerate exclusion of *anyone* under *any circumstances*. Each time I heard questions like that, I grew in my boldness to fight for the right of each person to sit in the pew, to feel the love of God and God's people, to be touched by God, and to experience a taste of the kingdom of God. As this conviction spread and permeated our church, people in our community realized that if they'd just walk through the door, they'd be welcomed with open arms. Authentic love, it seems, is pretty attractive to a lot of people.

Authentic love, it seems, is pretty attractive to a lot of people.

BEYOND SUPERFICIAL

As I continued to read the New Testament, one of the things that impressed me most about Jesus is that He took plenty of time to get to know lots of people—the powerful and the powerless, the slick and the sick. He went to their parties, dined with them, and engaged in lengthy conversations. And His deep involvement in their lives invoked the most caustic attacks by those who prided themselves in being clean and right. The Pharisees accused John the Baptist of being demon-possessed because John ate strange things, like bugs, but when Jesus ate and drank at parties with His friends, the Pharisees accused Him of being a drunk and a glutton. When

Jesus seemed to take special delight in showing up the rigid by showing love to the rejected.

He enjoyed time with outcasts, these religious leaders grumbled, "This man welcomes sinners and eats with them," as if it was the worst crime a person could commit. And when Jesus showed children special affection, His own disciples tried to correct Him. Nothing could prevent Jesus from showing love and acceptance to every person in His path, but He seemed to take special delight in showing up the rigid by showing love to the rejected.

But to be honest, I didn't come to that perspective about loving the unlovely in a vacuum. I learned it all from watching my Auntie Mae Mae as she ran her store, the Allen Food Market.

AUNTIE MAE MAE

Auntie Mae Mae ran a grocery store on 1714 Patterson Street in Houston. From the time I was a little boy, I watched her treat every person—from winos to suits—with dignity and respect. When I was about six years old, I started going to her store every afternoon after school and on weekends. She let me help by dusting the shelves. By the time I was ten, I often stood in a chair and worked the cash register. She not only taught me about love; she also taught me about business. She was a marvelous businesswoman! I sometimes tell people that I went to the Hattie Mae Allen School of Business. She was a remarkable woman.

Those hours in Auntie Mae Mae's store showed me the very best example of God's love that I've ever seen. Day after day, I watched her show kindness and bestow respect on people, even those who were outcasts in our community. I remember watching a drunk stumble through the front door, but before my aunt saw him, he tried to straighten up to look presentable because he wanted to be worthy of her love. Her unconditional love motivated him to be the best he could be at that moment. He came in to buy a little food. He didn't have much money, because he spent almost all of it on liquor, but he was a regular customer and bought whatever he could afford. Auntie Mae Mae treated him with the same respect she would have treated the mayor of Houston if he'd come in the store.

I believe people have built-in radar to detect the level of acceptance we offer them. We don't have to say we love them. They sense it. We don't have to make a sign that says we accept them the way they are. They know it instinctively. And it amazes them!

Auntie Mae Mae taught me that people respond to one another in one of two ways: in fear or in love. There may be a thousand subcategories, but these

Auntie Mae Mae taught me that people respond to one another in one of two ways: in fear or in love.

are the two primary responses in any situation. When the wino walked through the door of Allen Food Market, he knew my aunt's response to him wouldn't be fear. He could count on Auntie Mae Mae loving him. She wasn't afraid that he would try to steal something, that another customer would be offended by her acceptance of him, or that he might become too attached to her because he enjoyed her acceptance so much. All those things (and many others) were genuine risks and sometimes occurred, but she never let those possibilities cloud her commitment to show genuine acceptance and respect to each person who walked through her door. Her love conquered all fears.

Fear is at the heart of exclusion, and fear perpetuates our desire to be distant from people who aren't like us. But love is a tremendously powerful force. I know. I saw it in action. Auntie Mae Mae was an incredible lady. In addition to running her store, she worked for forty-seven years as the manager of a school lunchroom. After school each day, she went to the grocery store. From the time I was a little boy, I hung out at the store with her, and I watched her like a hawk. She didn't talk to her customers about love, but she modeled it all day every day. In fact, one of the things that was so amazing to me was her consistency. No matter how tired she was, and no matter how annoying a customer might be, Auntie Mae Mae treated each one as if he or she was the most important person in the world.

Her commitment to love people was honed, as it often is, in heartache.

Her commitment to love people was honed, as it often is, in heartache. Difficulties make us bitter or better, and Auntie Mae Mae's difficulties caused her to make a heartfelt and lifelong commitment to show love even to those who hurt her—like her husband. They were married for fifty years, and for most of those years, he abused her. I knew it was happening, and for some reason, I felt comfortable enough to ask her about it. Her reply was simply, "Little Rudy [my daddy was "Big Rudy"], he's my husband." In the midst of physical pain and emotional rejection, she went deep into the heart of God to find His love for her. Her intimate, rich experience of God's unconditional love gave her strength, and it caused her to see each person, including my uncle, with a fresh set of eyes. She was convinced that each man or woman, boy or girl was valuable—no matter what he'd done, no matter how she acted. She treated each person as a treasure. And every person sensed it.

The apostle John wrote, "Perfect love casts out fear" (1 John 4:18 NKJV). I saw that truth demonstrated every afternoon at Allen Food Market. Many of the people who came in scared me. They looked strange, smelled bad, and acted weird, but Auntie Mae Mae looked past all of that to see the intrinsic value of each person. She pushed aside any fears, and she showed love to them. When they asked a question, she stopped what she was doing and looked them in the eye as she smiled and responded. If they returned something they didn't need, she thanked them for coming in. When they were impatient, she never matched their level of intensity. She always (yes, *always*) showed kindness, grace, and love. She was the model Christian, the person in my mind who, even today, most clearly represents the love of Christ.

But don't get me wrong. Auntie Mae Mae was warm and kind, but she was tough as nails. She got really angry when she saw people suffer from injustice—especially if the victims of injustice were those she loved. Back in the '60s, racism

Auntie Mae Mae was warm and kind, but she was tough as nails. She got really angry when she saw people suffer from injustice.

and segregation were still prevalent in our country and in our city. One day my Aunt Norma, who was a college freshman when I was about nine, took me with her on a bus to downtown Houston. The bus stop was in front of Wolf's Pharmacy, one of the few white-owned businesses in our community. That was before the days of air-conditioned buses, and it was hot. We were tired and thirsty, and sweat was pouring off our faces, so we decided to go to Wolf's to get something to drink. Aunt Norma and I sat at the counter at the soda fountain. Mr. Wolf walked over and glared at us. We were just about to order a cold drink when he snarled, "No, you don't! You can't sit here." He pointed to a secluded area in the back and told us, "Nigras have to sit back there."

Aunt Norma was stunned. I didn't know exactly what was going on, but I could feel the tension between Mr. Wolf and us. I sensed Aunt Norma's fear. We immediately walked out the door and ran to the store to tell Auntie Mae Mae. She listened carefully, asked a few questions to clarify what happened, and then she picked up the phone. She dialed a number, and after a few seconds, she said, "I'd like to speak to Mr. Wolf, please." A moment passed before Mr. Wolf picked up the phone; then Auntie Mae Mae spoke in a clear, calm voice of unmistakable conviction: "Mr. Wolf, my nephew and my niece were just in your store. They told me you refused them a seat at the counter. I was not pleased to hear that. Mr. Wolf, you've been in this community for a long time. Virtually all of your cus-

Her deep love caused her to protect the helpless and despise injustice in any form.

tomers are friends and relatives of mine. If any of us ever experiences anything like this again, you can be sure that your business will be adversely affected in a significant way. Do I make myself clear, sir?"

She hadn't yelled, and she hadn't cursed. She never lost control or exhibited an outburst of emotion, and she didn't wilt under the pressure of the situation. Her deep love caused her to protect the helpless and despise injustice in any form. She spoke the truth plainly, and she promised consequences if Mr. Wolf didn't comply. That day, Mr. Wolf got the message, and from that day on, he treated each person who came into his store with respect.

In one of the most powerful and poignant messages in the Gospels,

Jesus told us that the measure of our commitment to Him is shown in our care for people who are in trouble: those who are hungry, thirsty, naked, sick, or in prison. Each of these people, Jesus informs us, represents Him. He said, "Assuredly, I say to you, inasmuch as you did it to one of the least of these My brethren, you did it to Me" (Matt. 25:40 NKJV). That day in Mr. Wolf's store, Aunt Norma and I represented "one of the least of these," the forgotten, the helpless, and the hopeless. We needed somebody to care for us—not just to feel sorry for us, but also to take action to defend us and restore our dignity. Auntie Mae Mae was our advocate, standing in the gap for us. That's what she did for us that day . . . and every day.

Auntie Mae Mae died several years ago, but I can still picture her today. She was a short, stout, tenacious, warm woman whose presence exuded the love and strength of Jesus Christ. When I became a believer, I had a wealth of experience watching someone whose heart was in tune with God's and who treated people a lot like Jesus treated them. Long before I came to faith, she was my real-world encounter with Christianity on a daily basis.

LESSONS FROM AISLE 1

I learned many wonderful lessons from Auntie Mae Mae—about business, about relationships, about God, and about life. Here are a few that stand out:

• *Engage before judging.*

We all have to make snap decisions every day: in traffic, about lunch, what to buy, what to watch or listen to, and thousands of other choices. But we need to make decisions about people much more slowly. Auntie Mae Mae refused to judge people by their first impression or initial appearance. She always got to know people. She asked if she could help, and she listened. Quite often, I've found that even a short but meaningful conversation completely changes my perception of a person, or at least it gives me a richer understanding of what's beneath the surface in that person's life.

• *Love before leaving someone's presence.*

Every person who walked in the door of the grocery store was treated as though he or she was the only human being on earth. Auntie Mae Mae looked into people's eyes, she asked questions, and she remembered previous conversations. You see, each conversation wasn't about her. It was about them. I try to follow her example and connect with as many people as possible every day. Yes, I'm busy, but my load isn't nearly as heavy as the one Jesus carried, and He seemed to find time to connect with people in rich, strong, personal ways. A number of people who attend our church have mental problems. They can be absorbing, but Auntie Mae Mae and Jesus gave me examples of people going out of their way to show special affection for those in desperate need.

> *Every person who walked in the door of the grocery store was treated as though he or she was the only human being on earth.*

• *Personal pain is fertile ground to learn to love.*

Most people who experience the heartache of abuse and the pain of injustice don't realize that they are in a position to learn life's most powerful lessons. The very pain they are experiencing is the classroom for them to learn far more about God's character and purposes than they ever imagined. Auntie Mae Mae certainly used her pain as a classroom, and I'm learning to use mine in the same way. When times are tough, we instinctively ask, "Why?" but we also need to ask, "What do you want me to learn from this, Lord?"

• *Real love requires defending the helpless.*

Love involves more than warm feelings, a nice smile, and a big hug. Auntie Mae Mae was an advocate for those who were in trouble. She never glossed over the truth about a person or a situation. When a person's world was caving in, she never flippantly said, "Oh, it's okay. Don't worry about it. I'm sure everything will be fine." And she never said, "It's not your fault" when someone needed to take responsibility for his behavior. She looked the facts squarely in the eye, and then she stepped up, spoke the truth, and took action. I've tried to follow her example by being brutally honest about people and circumstances, and then defending the rights of the helpless and hopeless against exclusion, racism, and all forms of injustice. That's my calling, but I'm not alone. All of us are called to the same kind of love for those around us.

REWARDS AND RISKS

Loving people and defending the helpless have their rewards. Sometimes I went to the school and watched the ladies who worked for Auntie Mae Mae in the school cafeteria. Some were black, some were white, and some were Hispanic, but they all loved and admired her. In fact, they were intensely loyal to her. She was both honest and kind, and people knew they could trust her. I saw that same response in the grocery store every day. Customers loved and trusted her, and to be honest, they sincerely admired her. That was a rich reward for her love for them.

Still more rewards are found when the challenge of loving some people (such as those who are bitter or annoying or threatening) forces us to seek fresh, rich experiences of the love of God. Auntie Mae Mae had felt pain in her life, but instead of lashing out in bitterness or wallowing in self-pity, she dug deeper into the heart of God and found a fountain of unconditional grace, kindness, and affection.

Auntie Mae Mae had felt pain in her life, but instead of lashing out in bitterness or wallowing in self-pity, she dug deeper into the heart of God and found a fountain of unconditional grace, kindness, and affection.

She had every reason to fear her husband, her customers, and crime in her community, but she muscled that fear aside and replaced it with attention and affection. (Actually, there were three things she was really afraid of: rats, frogs, and snakes, but who can blame her for that?)

When Hurricane Rita came barreling toward Houston in the fall of 2005, the roads were clogged with more than two million people who fled the city. For a couple of days, I thought and prayed about what to do. Some of my friends had left with their families to get away from the storm, and others had taken the last flights out. After a long time of anguishing prayer, I decided that Juanita and I would stay here. On the morning the hurricane sped like a freight train toward the city, I went downtown to the church. The streets of Houston were deserted, but the homeless people had nowhere to go. When I walked to the door of the church, two men came up behind me. I turned around, and one of them looked at me and said solemnly, "Pastor Rudy, we knew you wouldn't leave us." His statement to me that morning was a rich reward for my love and loyalty to people like him over the past dozen years. I made a commitment to treat each person with dignity. That means telling the truth, the plain, unvarnished truth, no matter how hard it is to hear it. And it means accepting each person—

from the sick and homeless to the rich and famous—with God's great love. They trust me, and that's a wonderful reward.

But caring for people the way Jesus cared also involves real risks. In equal measure to the admiration and loyalty we enjoy from those we love, our caring attitudes and actions evoke jealousy and hatred from some people around us. Jesus told His followers, "Blessed are you when they revile and persecute you, and say all kinds of evil against you falsely for My sake. Rejoice and be exceedingly glad, for great is your reward in heaven" (Matt. 5:11–12 NKJV).

Sometimes, the price of choosing love instead of fear is rejection. I wish it weren't so, but in the spirit of "truth in advertising," I need to be honest with you. I remember a few quiet moments with my aunt when she sadly told me, "Baby, I don't understand some of the people who come in the store. Even though I know they don't have money, I give them credit so they can buy the food they need. But when they get some money, they go down the street to another store." It broke her heart, not that she lost some business, but that her love was repaid with disloyalty. She felt betrayed. During times like these Auntie Mae Mae would tell me, "People can only do what they know to do."

> *But caring for people the way Jesus cared also involves real risks.* ★

What can we expect when we choose love over fear in relating to people? We can anticipate some of the richest, most meaningful interactions we've ever had, because people will pour out their hearts to us. We can expect most people to repay our love with trust and loyalty, but we can also expect a few to try to take advantage of our kindness, and a few of them will despise us. That's the range of people's responses to Jesus. Why should their response to us be any different?

Premeditated expectations often lead to disappointment, and then to resentment. Certainly, I hope each person responds to my love with joy and delight, but when my hope turns into a fixed expectation (which is another term for a demand), I get very disappointed with anything less than their complete love and loyalty in return. Disappointment, however, doesn't last long. If it isn't identified and resolved, it quickly turns to resentment. The thinking goes like this: *I treated you with love and respect, so I* deserve *for you to respond with appreciation.* That sense of entitlement—that we deserve a positive response—ruins our motivation and clouds our relationships.

Premeditated expectations often lead to disappointment, and then to resentment.

Ultimately, our reward for loving people isn't the positive response of those we love. It's the smile of God on our lives. Loving people and defending them against injustice is the overflow of a heart that is fixed on Christ and full of His love and strength. He delights in us representing Him this way, and His delight is our highest reward.

The first great revival recorded in the New Testament was sparked by a "fast woman" Jesus found by a well in Samaria. She responded to His truth, love, and acceptance, and she went back to town to spread the news about the Savior. While she was gone, the disciples were much more interested in lunch than a foreigner, but Jesus told them, "I have food to eat of which you do not know. . . . My food is to do the will of Him who sent Me" (John 4:32, 34). When we treat people the way God wants us to treat them, we are like Jesus, doing the will of Him who sent us. We have a clear conscience, a peaceful heart, and a genuine joy that comes from following our gracious God. There will come a day when we will give an account for everything we've done here on earth. On

Ultimately, our reward for loving people isn't the positive response of those we love. It's the smile of God on our lives.

that day, I think God is going to take a long, hard look at what we've done "with the least of these." There's little reward in giving to those who can give back to us, but God promises great reward if we will give, love, and serve those who can never repay us.

I came to faith in Christ by reading the Gospels to see what He was really like. I quickly realized He wasn't like the stained-glass guy carrying the lamb. He wasn't stiff and passive. He was full of passion and heart and humor and love. His life, though, was marked by irony: the most loving human being ever known was mocked, ridiculed, falsely accused, betrayed, abandoned, beaten, and murdered. The word *disciple* means "follower." When I decided to become a disciple of Jesus and follow Him, I knew I'd find the same irony in my own life. I'd enjoy seeing God use me to touch people's lives, but I'd also experience some of the same abuse and abandonment He experienced—not to the same degree, but of the same type. But Jesus endured the suffering "for the joy . . . set before Him" (Heb. 12:2 NKJV). That joy was the thrill of the Father's smile at His obedience, and the deep, lasting thrill of seeing the people's lives eternally changed because they sensed His touch.

> *There's little reward in giving to those who can give back to us, but God promises great reward if we will give, love, and serve those who can never repay us.*

When you and I choose to be followers of Jesus, it means we learn to love the way He loves. It's the most challenging and the most fulfilling journey life has to offer.

If it happened to J. It will happen to you.

MY HOPE FOR YOU

All of us long to love and be loved. This deep desire for authentic relationships is part of what it means to be created in God's image. We aren't robots. We need to be connected to people, but many of us look at our life's story and conclude that our painful experiences and poor choices prevent us from being loved and loving others. The good news is that this conclusion isn't true! In many ways, this book is autobiographical. It's the story of God touching the heart of a lost, broken, and selfish man and transforming him from the inside out. My hope is that you will conclude that God can do the same thing in your life. No matter how badly you've been hurt and no matter what you've done, God can use even your worst pain and your biggest sins as building blocks to construct something beautiful in your life. The first and most important step, though, is to open our hearts to the loving touch of Jesus. To the extent that we truly experience His love and touch, we'll be willing and able to express love to those around us, and especially those who don't love us back.

I can only point you to Jesus and encourage you to get real with Him. When that happens, a revolution takes place in your heart! It's a transformation that is more powerful and deep than any formula can promise.

Not long ago, I gave a message about the birth of Christ. I had been thinking of the baby Jesus being born in a back alley of a strange town. People didn't even know who His real daddy was. I asked the congregation, "How many of you were born 'in the 'hood'?" About two-thirds raised their hands. I told them, "That's where Jesus was born too." He identified with "the least of these" throughout His whole life, even from the moment of His birth.

Recently, I spent some time reading the first chapter of Matthew. I had always thought the list of Jesus' ancestors was really boring, but this time, I looked more carefully at the ancestors of our Savior. They aren't exactly a collection of angels! One was a hooker, another was a foreigner, and all of them were flawed . . . sometimes terribly flawed, but God used each of them to touch you and me. My conclusion was that if God could use them, He could use me, too. And He can use you. The only ones God doesn't use are those who are too proud to admit their need for His forgiveness, love, and strength.

God wants to use our darkness and failure, yours and mine, to soften our hearts and fill them with His grace and love so that He can use us to touch all kinds of people.

A lot of books offer "seven steps" or "a secret formula" to success. This book doesn't offer those kinds of things. I can only point you to Jesus and encourage you to get real with Him. When that happens, a revolution takes place in your heart! It's a transformation that is more powerful and deep than any formula can promise. Then, His love and strength flow through you to touch the hearts of hurting people around you—and in case you didn't know it, that includes everybody.

God isn't looking for perfect people to pour His love into and channel His love to others. He's looking for people who are willing to say, "Lord Jesus, here I am. I'm not much, but I'm all Yours. Touch me in the deepest place of my soul with Your matchless love. And, Lord, I invite You to use me to touch people around me."

The ancestors of Jesus experienced darkness, just as I have experienced it. They experienced colossal failure; I have, too. But God used their darkness and failure as stepping-stones to bring us the Savior. In the same way, God wants to use our darkness and failure, yours and mine, to soften our hearts and fill them with His grace and love so that He can use us to touch all kinds of people—the down-and-out and the up-and-coming, the hopeless and the proud—with authentic, transforming love.

THE IDEA OF CHANGE

My friend Christian Washington is a management consultant who has helped many executives and Christian leaders become more effective. One of his insights identifies specific elements in the dynamic process of change. He uses the acronym "IDEA" to help people remember and apply these principles, which apply equally well to individuals and groups of people. We have used this process very effectively at St. John's, and I want to use it as a guide for individual and group reflection in this book.[1] The four elements of IDEA are:

o *Information*—First, we need a basic understanding of the concepts, principles, and processes. This is the *current state* of our or our organization's condition.

o *Disturbance*—New information often challenges our assumptions and habits, and we experience a *chaotic state* in which we feel uncomfortable. Many people stop at this point and retreat back to safety, but if they keep going, genuine and productive change is possible.

o *Emergence*—Wrestling with new concepts or goals in the disturbance phase forces us to reflect more deeply and clearly. In this process, our thinking is *clarified* and new solutions emerge.

o *Adaptation*—At first, our specific steps of action may be faltering and hesitant, but each step builds confidence and effectiveness. Soon, the *change* becomes a normal part of life as the new paths become established as we develop new and effective habits.

Reading articles and books stimulates my thinking and teaches me important principles, but I've found that pointed questions and honest conversations with friends help me apply those principles in my own experience. Perhaps you will too. In this book, the Going Deeper Study Guide on page 221 contains questions for each of the chapters. These questions address all four elements of the IDEA model. We've provided some space for you to write your answers, but you may need a separate notebook for your reflections. Let me encourage you to spend a little extra time on the questions designed to produce disturbance. Honest answers to those questions open the door to real change.

Use these questions to reflect, pray, and consider how God wants to fill your life with His love so that His love overflows into your relationships with others. These questions are also designed to stimulate rich, meaningful discussions in small groups and leadership teams.

CHAPTER 2
Grace with Skin On

This is a faithful saying and worthy of all acceptance, that Christ Jesus came into the world to save sinners, of whom I am chief. (I TIMOTHY 1:15 NKJV)

Real and total freedom can only be found through downward mobility. —HENRI NOUWEN

Auntie Mae Mae showed me love in action, but my father's life demonstrated the powerful impact of fear. Don't get me wrong. His fear didn't compel him to cower and hide. It did the opposite. My dad was determined to never, ever let anybody get the best of him. His fear made him suspicious and propelled him toward self-protection in its strongest form—Dad always packed a gun.

When I was five years old, my father brought home a set of blueprints for a motel he intended to build. He explained in graphic detail how men and women would come to this place to have sex with people who weren't their spouses. I didn't understand all the details, but he wanted to tell me about it anyway. About twenty years later, we built the motel, and I joined him in the family business. The motel fulfilled all of his expectations. We rented rooms by the hour, and people came in droves to ruin their lives. Shortly after I joined him in the business, I took over the day-to-day operations. We didn't hire the girls—they were independent contractors. We just provided the rooms. For that reason, I called our business a "borderline bordello."

BEHIND THE ONE-WAY GLASS

The motel office had a one-way glass. It looked like a mirror to people in the lobby, but from the office, it was a window on the world. From where I sat, I saw some of the most amazing things ever witnessed in the city of Houston. I could tell story after story about what I observed every night, from bestiality to abuse. Politicians came to take advantage of our discreet location, and some preachers came too. Every conceivable sex act was committed in those rooms . . . including a few I never could have imagined. One night, one of the girls came running into my office. "Rudy," she panted, "Mr. Smith . . . Mr. Smith is really sick!" I ran with her back to the room. Mr. Smith wasn't sick—he was dead! He'd had a fatal heart attack. It was just another night at Motel Houston.

I called our business a "borderline bordello."

We were purveyors of darkness, and we destroyed people's lives for an hourly fee. During all these years before I met Christ, I don't know if I ever thought what we were doing was wrong. It was just the family business, kind of like the Corleones in *The Godfather*. In addition to the borderline bordello, I was also involved in several other businesses, including real estate. I wanted to make as much money as possible. Wealth, I was convinced, was the ticket to the good life.

After a few years of success in the business, I met the beautiful young woman who would make an everlasting impact on my life. Actually, I first saw Juanita at a funeral. She was sitting on the far side of the crowd, and I spent the entire service trying to figure out how to meet her. After the service I met her mother (a shrewd maneuver on my part), and she introduced us. Immediately, I could tell that Juanita was sharp—really sharp. We started dating, and I made a point of not hiding anything from her. I told her I ran the motel, and I guess my honesty was attractive to her. She had a strong walk with God. That was fine with me, but I wasn't interested in God in the least. My full attention was on Juanita and the perfect "life partner" she would make for me. If she brought God along as part of the deal, I could live with that.

After a few years of success in the business, I met the beautiful young woman who would make an everlasting impact on my life.

After Juanita and I were married and began our family, she wanted me to go to church with her. Somehow I knew that was the right thing to do, so I began attending Windsor Village United Methodist Church each week. For a long time I went, because that's what good husbands and fathers do. We'd go to church, greet our church friends, and then drive back to the motel where we lived. I was as far out on the margins of faith as anyone could be.

During this period, I kept watching Juanita. Like Auntie Mae Mae, she lived a consistent, strong Christian life in front of me day after day. When times were good, we enjoyed them together. When times were tough, she was supportive. Her love never wavered, not one bit. She never nagged me about going to church, and she never tried to coerce me to become a Christian. She just loved me unconditionally, and she prayed. She had lots of reasons to give up on me, because for so long, I simply didn't care about God. But somehow, God gave her the faith to believe that He was going to work in my life. At that time, Juanita was praying Psalm 1:1 for me, and she put my name in the verse as she prayed for me for the next five years. She made me a puzzle to remind me of God's great purpose for my life.

Juanita patiently and persistently loved me in the same way that Auntie Mae Mae loved her husband. The only difference is that my aunt ran out of time and didn't see her husband respond to her love. Juanita saw her love for me make a dent . . . and then make a difference.

By 1991, I had attended church at Windsor Village for a couple of years. One Sunday, Pastor Kirbyjon Caldwell invited all the men to come together on a Wednesday night. I decided to go. After some introductory comments, he asked everybody to divide up into groups according to their parts of town. I had no idea this was going to happen, but a man named Willie Lane got us together in our designated corner of the room and invited us to a weekly Bible study. Their method of getting my commitment to join a Bible study seemed a bit slick to me, but I decided that joining this group was cool.

THE LIGHTS COME ON

We began the next Thursday night at a little restaurant called Jade Hawaii on Main Street in Houston. Each week for an entire year, Willie opened the Bible, read a passage, and we discussed it. I didn't miss a single time. The owner of the restaurant gave us a room with a big table and let us sit there for hours each week.

By the end of that year, Willie's teaching and his patient answers to my questions resulted in the lights coming on in my heart. I trusted Jesus Christ to be my Savior. (It wasn't until much later that I realized that Willie had discipled me by loving me into the kingdom. He was a real gift from God.) I had heard the gospel story my whole life. As a child, I had gone to Sunday school, vacation Bible school, and church, but I hadn't bought what they were selling. The stories were nice, but they didn't make any difference to me. But in those Thursday night talks with Willie and the other men, I looked into the tomb myself, and I found that it was really empty. That's what Peter and John did when they heard the report that Jesus had been raised from the dead. They had to see for themselves, so they ran to the tomb and looked inside. For the first time in my life, I felt peace, and as a result, I began to respond to God and people in love instead of fear.

My dad had taught me to be suspicious of everybody because he was convinced that people were trying to con him. He was often right; some of them were. But his accurate observation about a few became a blanket suspicion about everybody. It was these fears that prompted him to carry a gun, and he was always ready to use it. In fact, he told me, "Never pull out your gun unless you're ready to shoot somebody." Not surprisingly, I also carried a gun for many years.

As I experienced more of God's touch in my life, His love melted or muscled out my fear of people. Instead of guarding myself against them, I started to care about them. I began to act more like Auntie Mae Mae and Juanita, and that was a real miracle. But my new behavior looked really strange to people who knew me. I was living in a world dominated by fear. Self-protection and suspicion were standard operating procedure; love and trust were intruders. In the world of fear, you're always looking over your shoulder to find the ones who are trying to take what's yours, or you wonder if people will try to get revenge because they think you've taken something from them. But in the world of love, all of that changes. We're not looking at others with suspicion, but with eyes to see needs so we can meet them. It's radical. It's revolutionary. And it's really odd. People who knew me started talking to each other. They shook their heads and told one another, "What's up with Rudy? There's something different about him."

Jesus was convincing me that He wanted me to live for Him: completely, totally, and absolutely. That was the only reasonable response to His sacrifice for me. As my heart changed, my values changed. I lived in a world of guns, drugs, and prostitution, where fear was almost palpable. But now, instead of being afraid of people, I had a new, fresh, totally unrehearsed reverence for God. A passage of Scripture that meant a lot to me during that time was where Jesus taught people, "Do not fear those who kill the body but cannot kill the soul. But rather fear Him who is able to destroy both soul and body in hell" (Matt. 10:28 NKJV). In the world of darkness, fear is real for a reason: there's plenty to be afraid of. But God's work in my heart—His power, truth, and grace—was even more real. He began to dominate my thoughts, my feelings, and my choices.

In the world of fear, you're always looking over your shoulder to find the ones who are trying to take what's yours.

In my first year as a Christian, our family was still living in the motel, and I continued to run the family business, but God was at work in my heart. Gradually, my conscience came alive, and I realized I couldn't continue to run this business and consider myself a Christian. One of my father's guiding principles was "Don't play with God." He wasn't a believer yet, but he knew better than to take the Almighty for granted. I knew I couldn't keep running the business and claim to follow Jesus. That would be playing with God, and He wouldn't stand for that. Day after day, I sensed a gravitational pull to help people, and ruining their lives by facilitating illicit sex wasn't helping them! Something had to change.

One of my father's guiding principles was "Don't play with God."

I really began to "cross over to the good side" on a particular day at a particular moment. I remember it as if it was yesterday. One of our most reliable customers was a man (actually, he was a pastor) who drove up to the motel at the same time on the same day every week. I could always count on this man regularly dropping some money with us. That day when he parked his truck, I felt compelled to say something to him. I walked out to the parking lot, and as he got out, I leaned forward and blurted out, "Man, why are you doing this? Why are you ruining your life?" He was shocked, and to be honest, so was I! I had a car note to pay, and I couldn't afford to turn away paying customers, especially our most loyal ones.

In an instant, guilt and shame covered his face. But almost as quickly, his lust for sex overcame his shame, and he walked past me to have his hour of pleasure. The confrontation made him feel uncomfortable, but he gave in to sex. It made me feel uncomfortable too, but I gave in to the opposite force at work that day: to the transforming power of God's touch. From that moment on, I sensed God was calling me away from the family business and into ministry.

About the same time, Kirbyjon asked me to read the liturgy at church one Sunday. I wondered why in the world he would ask somebody like me to read in a worship service, but I agreed to do it. He knew what my life was like. I hadn't hidden anything from him, but God prompted him to ask me to read. When I stood up in front of the church, an amazing thing happened: the roof didn't fall in, the altar didn't melt, and the pulpit didn't catch on fire. But even more incredible was the clear, powerful sense of God's Spirit at work in my heart. When I got back to the motel that afternoon, a friend noticed that something in the core of my being was different. I had changed. God had touched me at a deeper level. And that change took me another step in my heartfelt desire to not only *do right*, but to *do good* for our community.

AN UNMISTAKABLE CALLING

At the end of my first year as a Christian, the sense of God's calling in my life was so strong that I began telling people that God had called me to ministry. First, I told two pastors at Windsor Village, Joe Palmore and Thad Eastland. They easily could have laughed at me, or they could have put up a thousand roadblocks in my path because they thought I wasn't qualified. But they didn't. They were very affirming and kind, and they explained what it meant to be a minister in our denomination.

I had gotten to know Kirbyjon Caldwell in the years I'd been attending Windsor Village, and I had the greatest respect for him. In those years, he had asked me to serve as his real estate broker, so I really got to know the man. He was authentic. The more I got to know him, the more I realized this guy didn't play games with God or with people. He spoke the truth, and he was the same man in his private conversations with me that he was when he spoke to thousands. As I mentioned, one of my father's rules was: "never trust preachers and church folk," so I had a built-in suspicion about all preachers. That's why my time with Kirbyjon impressed me so much. He wasn't at all like the preachers my father had warned me about.

I scheduled an appointment to see Kirbyjon, and I told him that

I felt that God had called me to the ministry. I'll never forget his response. He leaned back in his chair, looked at me, and asked, "Why do you want to do that?"

His question caught me off guard, and it took me years to understand what he was really asking me that day. He wasn't questioning God's work in my heart, but he knew that being involved in ministry requires far more sacrifice than most people can imagine. I'm not talking about just financial sacrifice, though that's part of it. I knew I'd be making far less money than I was currently making. But the real sacrifices involve the enormous pressures on the minister's time, the pressure on his family, and the temptations to institutionalize his ministry instead of keeping it fresh and real. Kirbyjon understood these sacrifices very well, and his question probed my grasp of them. At the time, I didn't get it at all. That understanding wouldn't come until much later.

One of my father's rules was: "Never trust preachers and church folk," so I had a built-in suspicion about all preachers.

Not long after that meeting with Kirbyjon, he asked me to speak on Laity Sunday. I agreed and gave the message on October 15, 1991. I have no idea if what I said that day made any sense at all, but people were very kind to me. Lots of them came up to tell me what a great job I'd done. I have a picture of our family that day. I was standing at the altar with Juanita, holding my little girls in my arms. I'm not sure if anybody else was blessed by my message that day, but I was. God used it to confirm His calling in my life.

I spoke only two other times that first year after God called me to ministry. Both of these were at the church pastored by the man who was a regular customer at the motel—the same pastor I confronted in the parking lot. For reasons known only to God, he asked me to preach at his church. The first time, I brought everybody I knew, family and friends, to hear me. My guests even outnumbered the rest of his little congregation. The offering that day was so good that he asked me to come back again.

ST. JOHN'S

In the summer of '92, the denomination contacted Kirbyjon and asked him to take another church under his leadership. St. John's was a failing church in the heart of Houston, located next to the Pierce Elevated section of I-45 downtown. Since I was his real estate broker, he asked me to check out the building. I drove across town and parked my car in front of the church. As soon as I stopped, I had a clear, unmistakable sense that this was the place God was calling me to minister. I picked up my cell phone and called Juanita. I told her in a voice that probably sounded like a six-year-old at Christmas, "Baby, this is the place!" She knew immediately what I was talking about. All of my life's experiences suddenly came together and made sense. In that instant, all the pieces fit.

"Baby, this is the place!"

I looked around, and the only people I could see in every direction were homeless people. For a reason that can only be a mark of God's calling in my life, I immediately felt right at home. Two homeless men, Kelly and Maurice, walked up to me and offered to show me around. Those men became two of my closest friends, and they were powerfully effective links to the homeless community in Houston. I later called these guys "my homeless consultants."

After looking around the building, I called Kirbyjon and told him, "I think we can do something here." Before long, he asked me to establish a ministry at St. John's. I wasn't a licensed pastor, and I wasn't ordained by our denomination. Kirbyjon, though, recognized that God had called me to serve Him, so he asked me to take a leadership role at St. John's.

Within weeks, we had taken over the building and cleaned it up. When we arrived, there were nine members of the church, and they were very gracious to Juanita and me. They knew their church was dying, and they were happy to have some fresh vision, enthusiasm, and activity to serve God there. The original nine members of the church were all elderly white people, at an average age of about seventy. These dear people had shown a lot of heart during the decline of the church. For a long time, they had paid the electric and water bills out of their own pockets just to keep the place going. Now they welcomed black people to lead their church in a new direction. I've heard it said that old white people are stuck in their ways, but these people were revolutionaries with open hearts. They loved God, and they loved us for helping revitalize their church.

About fifty people from Windsor Village came over to help us jump-start the church, and we held our first service on the first Sunday in September. In addition to the nine original members and the people from Windsor, some homeless people joined us that first Sunday.

I hadn't been trained to be a preacher, so every week Juanita and I led the service until it was time for the sermon. Often with only a few minutes to spare, Kirbyjon came in from across town and delivered the message. As soon as he was done, he handed the microphone back to me and he ran back out the door to Windsor Village. Every Sunday, he preached three services at his campus and one at St. John's. That hectic pace couldn't last too long, but he kept it up for four months so we could get established. He was a tremendous gift to us.

THE TIPPING POINT

By the second week in October, Juanita and I had joined in the preaching rotation to give Kirbyjon a break. For a while, he spoke at St. John's only once a month. Almost from the beginning, Kirbyjon gave us complete freedom to create the kind of environment we felt necessary to make people in our community feel comfortable in church. We were determined to be a "no barriers" church, so our dress code was casual. I'm not talking about *normal* casual. We were committed to *radical* casual attire. Some churches say, "Come as you are," but that offer has real meaning when you minister to drug addicts, prostitutes, and homeless people. Everyone was welcome—no questions asked.

Kirbyjon gave us complete freedom to create the kind of environment we felt necessary to make people in our community feel comfortable in church.

To meet the obvious needs in our community, we began serving a meal to hungry people right after we opened the doors of the church. Some members that had come over from Windsor Village were instrumental in this effort. Jonathan and Connie Gregory and Pat and Helen Patterson were two pioneering couples who came to St. John's with a real commitment to serve. They embraced the mission to feed people. Once a week, we cooked in the kitchen and brought the food down to feed people in the sanctuary. The pews became our dining tables. From the beginning, we served about two hundred people per meal, and we called this ministry "Bread of Life." We funded many of the early meals and repairs to the church on Connie and Jonathan's credit card.

Then, something incredible happened. Author and cultural critic Malcolm Gladwell says that organizations sometimes experience "tipping points" when something happens that propels them to the next level of effectiveness.[1] In January, a religion reporter for the *Houston*

Chronicle heard about our ministry of serving meals in the sanctuary. He came to see us, interviewed us, and wrote an article a few days later. The article was the feature for the religion section; the title was "Downtown Church Feeds the Homeless." The article covered almost the entire front page of the religion section and continued for three more pages inside. It had lots of pictures, descriptions, and quotes, and it showed Juanita and me in blue jeans serving people in our sanctuary. The article explained that we were very casual so that every person would feel at home with us. That article was the tipping point, and it opened the floodgates. The very next Sunday, hundreds of people came to our church to experience God's love in an atmosphere that was caring and casual. St. John's growth really started that day, and it has continued ever since. But we're not trying to attract people from other churches. We reach out to people other churches don't want, or to people who, for some reason, don't feel comfortable in other churches. Here at St. John's, rejects feel accepted, outcasts feel included, and the shamed feel loved.

We reach out to people other churches don't want, or to people who, for some reason, don't feel comfortable in other churches.

For the first year at St. John's, I met with Kirbyjon every week for him to mentor me in spiritual life and ministry. That was an amazing privilege. Every Wednesday morning, we had breakfast together, and I gave him an update about our ministry. We talked about how God was working in people's lives, and we discussed how real ministry takes place in a church. He gave me advice on how to handle certain situations. He has a gift for looking into a complicated situation and seeing what is really happening. That's incredibly valuable in any context, but especially in the complexity of ministry. Meeting with him was the best education a young minister could possibly have. He completely empowered me and encouraged me to make my own decisions. One of the things I appreciated was that if anybody complained to him about me, he immediately sent that individual back to me to resolve the problem. He was unwilling for gossip to drive a wedge between us and ruin our relationship and the ministry God was building. The man has integrity. That's what was so attractive when I began attending Windsor Village before I was a believer, and my appreciation of his integrity only grew as I spent more time with him. Both of us were in business before we were in ministry, but at this point, he had been in ministry for eight or nine years. I learned everything I know about ministry from Kirbyjon.

RECRUITS

Jesus didn't see the sick, the lame, the blind, and the demon-possessed as a hindrance to His ministry. These people *were* His ministry. When He was criticized for caring for them, He replied that the very reason He came was to heal the sick, not hang out with those who are well, and to show mercy to every person who needed to be touched by God's love (see Matthew 9:9–13).

Many of the people who have received ministry from us have become volunteers who provide services for others. No, they may not fit the ideal list of criteria for volunteers, but they are our people, and they are doing a great job.

God hadn't called us to step over the poor, the homeless, the addicted, the prostitutes, and all the other people around St. John's. God was calling us to invite them in and show them mercy. But that's not all. These people weren't just going to be recipients of our ministry—they were to become ministers themselves. We asked homeless people to help us with marketing by telling other men and women who sleep under the bridges to come for a meal and to be loved. We asked a few of them to provide security for the church to be sure things remained safe and calm around the church. Many of these people are highly educated. Several have master's degrees, and a couple of them have PhD's. They've just fallen on hard times and need a place to regroup. Many of the people who have received ministry from us have become volunteers who provide services for others. No, they may not fit the ideal list of criteria for volunteers, but they are our people, and they are doing a great job.

DAD'S DISAPPOINTMENT

Through my journey as a Christian, certain passages of Scripture have held tremendous meaning for me. One of these is when Jesus told His followers, "Do not think that I came to bring peace on earth. I did not come to bring peace but a sword. For I have come to 'set a man against his father, a daughter against her mother, and a daughter-in-law against her mother-in-law'; and 'a man's enemies will be those of his own household'" (Matt. 10:34–36 NKJV). I had always been very close to my father. We were friends and business partners, but when I chose to walk with Christ, all of that changed.

I guess you could say that my dad was a complex man. He was a natural-born hustler, but he was ruthlessly honest. He was suspicious of others, but I trusted him completely. All my life, I listened to him because he had clear views about life. Here are a few of the lessons I learned from him:

o "Telling the truth may be painful, but you don't have to remember what you said the last time." (Dad never lied to me, regardless to the consequences.)

- "A good pair of boots makes it easier to wade through the bull-s_ _t." (Dad owned seventeen pairs of cowboy boots.)

- "Never pull out your gun unless you are ready to shoot somebody." (Dad always carried a gun and insisted that I did too.)

- "When your head is in the lion's mouth, don't scratch his behind." He really said "a_ _." (Dad insisted on knowing his situation so he could respond accordingly.)

- "Most folks are only *playing* crazy." (Dad never believed people were as crazy as they seemed. He was always watching for a con.)

- "Help somebody whenever opportunity presents itself, and never seek credit for it." (Dad would go out of his way to help family and friends.)

- "Laziness will kill you." (He said this whenever people attempted shortcuts that could lead to problems.)

- "If you're sick, people will care for two weeks, then you're on your own." (Dad noticed that after two weeks of illness, people returned to their daily routines and stopped visiting sick people.)

- "Never play with God." (Though he wasn't a committed believer for a long time, he respected God's rule and authority.)

Dad always complimented people who did things for him, but he was tough on lazy people. He cussed like a sailor, but he always asked church folk to pray for him. He had an incredible work ethic, but he was always smiling and never met a stranger. He kept secrets as if he was a Soviet agent, but he laughed a lot. He negotiated everything to get the best possible price, but he always made sure that Mom had the best of everything. When I needed advice, I turned to my dad.

When I needed money, I went to him. When times were hard and when times were good, I looked to him as my role model.

That's why it hurt so bad that he was bitterly disappointed that I chose to follow Christ. I felt tremendous tension as I tried to walk with God while I was running a borderline bordello. When it finally got to the breaking point, I told Dad, "I just can't keep running the business. I've got to get out."

He responded with a choice expletive, and in disgust told me, "Juanita prayed you into this s__t, didn't she?" And he turned and walked away. For the next three years, he told his friends that he had "lost Little Rudy to God." He had always taught me not to trust preachers and church folk, *"Juanita prayed you into this s__t, didn't she?"* and now he was confronted with the painful fact that I had become one of those people he never trusted. Dad felt abandoned and betrayed. He felt tremendous loss, and so did I.

Our relationship instantly changed from warmth and respect to strain and distance. He had poured his whole life into me and our business, and now I was turning my back and walking away. Ironically, not long after I left the motel, he closed the business, and we converted the property into a drug rehab facility, which was the ultimate redemption for that piece of property.

EVEN DAD

Those years of being estranged from my dad were some of the hardest of my life. But in that same passage in Matthew that I just mentioned, Jesus told us, "He who loves father or mother more than Me is not worthy of Me. And he who loves son or daughter more than Me is not worthy of Me" (10:37 NKJV). Yeah, I believed that.

I had chosen Jesus over my father, but my father's disappointment in me still hurt. It hurt a lot.

After a couple of years, a strange and wonderful thing happened. One Sunday, I saw a familiar figure walking into the church at St. John's. It was Dad! For the next several years, he came every Sunday for the eight o'clock service. He didn't say much, but he was there. Then one day, I heard from one of Dad's friends that he had said, "Well, I finally found a preacher I could trust." That comment did more for me than you can imagine. Later I heard that he'd said he was really proud of me because I hadn't taken advantage of people to gain more power and prestige as a pastor. For somebody who was suspicious of preachers, that was high praise!

Later I heard that he'd said he was really proud of me because I hadn't taken advantage of people to gain more power and prestige as a pastor.

He had raised me to love to make business deals, so every now and then, Dad tested my integrity by presenting me with an attractive but slightly shady deal. If I bit on it, he would know I'd gone back over to the dark side. After I turned down a few of these offers, he realized I had made a rock-solid commitment to serve God with integrity. At that point, he stopped testing me and started protecting me. He was now convinced that what God was doing in my life was real.

For six years, Dad came to church at St. John's every week. Then one Sunday, with no advanced warning or even a hint, he came forward and trusted Christ as his Savior. What a day! It was one of the biggest thrills of my life. My dad, who had been so suspicious of my commitment to God, experienced God's forgiveness himself. For me, it was a quiet validation that if my dad responded to God at least partially because of the changes he saw in me, those changes must be the real deal.

LOOKING BACK

[handwritten: Not why They left - why They Stay? Love]

Not long ago, we conducted a survey at St. John's to see why people were attending our church. The results might surprise you: 67 percent said they come because they feel loved. No other response came close. I thought that factor would be high, but it surprised even me. Why did so many people respond this way? They are as suspicious as my dad and as tough as I had been. Like every other human being on God's earth, they long to love and be loved, but they don't want something phony. They want the real thing, so it has to be authentic. By the grace of God, that's what they've found at St. John's.

The most amazing thing in the universe is that almighty God has been using me to help create this environment. Like the apostle Paul, I considered myself the "chief of sinners." Before I could be a channel for the grace of God, I had to experience it first. Nobody on God's green earth expected Rudy Rasmus to be touched by the love of God, but I was. Jesus didn't appear to me in a vision or a dream, but He showed Himself to me through the strong love of a few people: Auntie Mae Mae, Momma, Juanita, Willie Lane, and Kirbyjon Caldwell. They were God's grace with skin on. I told my story in this chapter not to glamorize my sin of profiting from the trade of personal destruction, but because I want to magnify the grace of God.

Pastor A. W. Tozer, author of *The Pursuit of God*, observed, "Seldom does God use a person greatly who has not been hurt deeply." Some of us are hurt by others, some by tragic circumstances, and some by our own actions. Deep wounds open our hearts to God's great healing, the kind that transforms every fiber of our being

> *[In a survey,] 67 percent said they come because they feel loved. No other response came close. I thought that factor would be high, but it surprised even me.*

so that we gladly give up everything to follow Him. That's what happened to me. If God is using me greatly, it is only because I realized—it took a long time, but I finally got it—that I wasn't the strong, self-sufficient man I thought I was. No, I was weak and afraid, desperately needy and wounded. Like the old hymn says, "It's me, it's me, it's me, O Lord, standing in the need of prayer."

He showed Himself to me through the strong love of a few people: Auntie Mae Mae, Momma, Juanita, Willie Lane, and Kirbyjon Caldwell. They were God's grace with skin on.

A deep and genuine grasp of the reality of our sins is the only path to a rich appreciation of God's forgiveness. Our depravity is the black velvet that shows off the brilliance of the diamond of God's grace. As I look at my life, I'm amazed that God would love and forgive somebody like me. I hope I'm always amazed at His mercy. It's the only right response.

Loving others is the second commandment, not the first. Jesus said the first commandment is to love God with all our heart, mind, and strength. We can't manufacture love for God. We can only be honest about our desperate need for His forgiveness and respond to His love for us. John wrote, "We love Him because He first loved us" (1 John 4:19 NKJV). Out of the deep well of that experience, God's love flows through us into the lives of others. If we aren't loving people, perhaps we haven't experienced enough of God's love ourselves. And the reason for our limited ability to love might be that we live in fear and try to protect ourselves from being hurt again.

I believe God reaches out to each one of us with a warm smile to invite us to receive His great love and forgiveness. The more we open our hearts and receive these gifts, the more we'll be willing and able to love those around us: spouse and children, best friends, annoying people, those whom we admire, and those who have wrecked their lives. The true test of our love is our affection and action to help "the least of these," who can never repay our kindness, but our wells run dry pretty quickly unless they are being replenished by the constant flow of God's love in our own experience.

Don't miss what I'm saying here. This, I'm convinced, is the most important point in this book. There's not a formula or a system to give us "five steps to loving God and people." It's a matter of the heart. When God gives us insight into our own rotten sinfulness—whether we've been obviously bad or self-righteously thought we were better than "those people"—we must go to Him with empty hands and open hearts. To the extent that we experience His grace, forgiveness, kindness, and love, we will respond by loving Him and loving others—even those who don't love us.

We sometimes talk about "sacrifice" and "hard choices" in following Jesus, and, yes, following Him requires some tough decisions. But there's another side that we often forget. Jesus told a brief parable about a man who found a treasure in a field. The treasure in the parable is Christ Himself. How did the man respond? With grim determination? Not at all. Jesus tells us, "And for joy over it he goes and sells all that he has and buys that field" (Matt. 13:44 NKJV). The treasure was so valuable that nothing else came close! If we have even the smallest grasp of the love, forgiveness, and kindness of God, we will treasure Him so much that we'll gladly make choices to value Him above all else. The apostle Paul had the same perspective about the joy of find-

> *The true test of our love is our affection and action to help "the least of these," who can never repay our kindness, but our wells run dry pretty quickly unless they are being replenished by the constant flow of God's love in our own experience.*

ing Christ, but his language was a bit more graphic. In his letter to the Philippians, he recounted his high position of prestige and influence before he was a believer, but when he met Christ, those things he had treasured so much seemed worthless in comparison. He wrote, "But what things were gain to me, these I have counted loss for Christ" (Phil. 3:7 NKJV). The translators used the word *loss*, but in the original language, the word means feces, dung, poop, crap, and of course, doo-doo (we'll stop there!).

Today, I try to relate to people in the opposite way that they expect from a church leader.

Compared to the incomparable value of being loved and loving Jesus, everything else life has to offer is no more valuable than doo-doo. Think about it.

Today, I try to relate to people in the opposite way that they expect from a church leader. Many people expect preachers to manipulate them to give or serve or attend, but I intentionally don't do that. I do my best to treat each individual with respect. That blows their minds. They are afraid I'll use them, but I choose to love them.

AS YOU LOOK BACK

Each of us has a story to tell. Not all of us have run bordellos, and not everybody has done something dramatically evil, like committing murder or selling drugs. The darkness in some of our lives is bitterness and resentment, the kind of hatred that Jesus said is just like murder in our hearts. Do you sense your own need—a desperate need—for God's forgiveness and kindness? I sure hope so. I sense it every day.

Every significant relationship and every experience is a classroom to teach us valuable lessons. From some people, like Auntie Mae Mae, we learn to love God and people no matter what. From others, like my dad, the lessons are more complicated. From him, I learned the value of hard work, honesty, and shrewd business practices. But for most of my life, dad didn't trust people outside the family, not even those who had proven to be trustworthy. In that way, his example was a negative one, but even negative examples can teach us valuable lessons.

As you look back at your own experiences, you can learn some important lessons from those who were good role models, and you can learn equally important lessons by observing poor models in your life. God has given you both for a reason. Pay attention. Author Henri Nouwen observed, "The dance of life finds its beginnings in grief. . . . Here a completely new way of living is revealed. It is the way in which pain can be embraced, not out of a desire to suffer, but in the knowledge that something new will be born in the pain."

God wants to use our darkness and failure, yours and mine, to soften our hearts and fill them with His grace and love so that He can use us to touch all kinds of people.

Don't discount the trauma you've experienced. You can learn incredible lessons from these heartaches, and you may find that God's purpose for you is shaped and crystallized by those events. C. S. Lewis said, "Pain is God's megaphone." He uses it to get our attention. God uses our pain to deepen our dependence on Him so we move past fear and we learn to live in love. When we experience God's love, we can lower our guard of self-protection, and we can really love people.

CHAPTER 3
He Touched Them

But He put them all outside, took her by the hand and called, saying, "Little girl, arise." Then her spirit returned, and she rose immediately. (LUKE 8:54–55 NKJV).

Let us touch the dying, the poor, the lonely and the unwanted according to the graces we have received, and let us not be ashamed or slow to do the humble work. —MOTHER TERESA

An orthopedic surgeon who practices near Houston told a friend of mine that God was doing something deep and challenging in his heart. He explained, "For years, I performed surgery on all kinds of patients. Some of them, to be blunt, stank. When these people came to my office before and after surgery, I'd treat their medical problem, but I got in and out of the examining room as quickly as possible, and except for the medical examination, I avoided touching them. About a year ago, I was reading the Gospels about Jesus touching lepers, lame people, blind people, and all kinds of sick people. My heart was shattered. Those people He touched were the same kinds of people who come to my office every day. From that day on, I've made a point of giving big, long hugs to every person—especially the smelly ones—who come to see me." Before God worked in his heart, this surgeon wasn't alone in his desire to avoid sick and needy people. Most of us want to stay as far away from them as possible, and we carefully construct our lives to keep our distance.

We live in an increasingly disconnected society. Most of us are incredibly busy and mobile, always rushing from one place to another. We might carve out a little time for someone, but then we hurry off to the next thing on our agenda. With the Internet and cell phones, we spend less and less time in face-to-face contact with people, and even when we're talking to people, we're thinking about the next thing we have to do. From news sources, the flood of information overwhelms our senses. We simply can't process all the facts coming at us—murders, cancer, hurricanes, war, job loss, divorce, abuse—so we gradually become emotionally numb. A song called "The News" by Jack Johnson describes a mother's attempts to shield her child from the brutal realities in the news. She tries to tell her child that the deaths and destruction they see aren't really true—they're just make-believe. But she realizes something is missing in the telecast. She asks:

"Why don't the newscasters cry when they read about the people who die?

You'd think they could be decent enough to put just a tear in their eyes."[1]

Many of us are overwhelmed by the sheer mass of violence and destruction in the news, and the effect is that we've become anesthetized, numb to the needs around us. We don't allow the needs we see on television—or the needs we hear about at dinner with our families—to touch our hearts.

INTENTIONAL

Physical touch has the power to comfort, affirm, and heal—and even the power of life and death. After World War II, a devastated Europe tried to care for thousands of orphans. The numbers, however, overwhelmed the caretakers. They only had time for the bare necessities of changing diapers and feeding the infants in their care, but for many of these infants, the absence of touch proved tragic. Many of them experienced severe symptoms of sensory deprivation, such as delayed physical development and stunted social development, and an alarming number of them actually died. A similar phenomenon was observed in Romanian orphanages after the fall of Nicolae Ceausescu in 1989. In the years before he was captured and executed, the dictator tried to double the population of his country to increase the country's economic power. Parents, though, couldn't care for all their children, so about 150,000 were put into orphanages where they suffered the effects of neglect. Approximately two-thirds of children under two years old experienced "Failure to Thrive" (delayed growth, low body weight, and failure to accomplish typical childhood milestones) caused by neglect, including the absence of physical touch.[2]

Physical touch has the power to comfort, affirm, and heal—and even the power of life and death.

In their outstanding book, *The Blessing*, Gary Smalley and John Trent draw a parallel between the Old Testament patriarchs' blessing their sons and the ways we can bless our own children. One of the five principles they identify is "meaningful touch." The power of touch, though, goes far beyond our own families. As we read the New Testament, we see Jesus reaching out to touch all kinds of people in need. No one was off-limits. He was intentional about extending His hands to make contact with people the religious leaders avoided like the plague.

One of my favorite accounts in the Gospels (and one the Gospel writers must have liked too, because three of them include it) is the story of Legion, the Gadarene demoniac. I identify with him. He lived among the tombs, isolated from the rest of the world—I lived at an isolated motel propagating human destruction. He inflicted pain on himself by "cutting himself with stones"—my choices inflicted pain on others and myself. Even when Legion's chains were broken, he stayed among the dead in the tombs. So too, when my own chains of doubt were broken, I continued to live at the motel for a while and run the business. Change is threatening. It's much easier to stay where things are familiar. People in Alcoholics Anonymous explain why they choose to continue destructive habits when they observe, "It may be hell, but at least I know the names of the streets."

He was intentional about extending His hands to make contact with people the religious leaders avoided like the plague.

Jesus was enjoying a time of popularity. Thousands of people were coming to hear Him, but in the middle of this acclaim, He told His disciples, "Let's go over to the other side of the lake" (Luke 8:22 NIV). After a stormy crossing, the boat arrived on the far shore. As Jesus and His men got out of the boat, Legion was standing at the edge of the water, naked, bleeding, posessed by demons, and smelling like death. Jesus cast the demons into a herd of pigs and set the tortured man free.

We usually find Jesus touching the sick, lame, blind, and demon-possessed, but He also touched those who were desperate for other reasons. When Peter saw Jesus walk on water, the big fisherman wanted to try it too. He stepped out of the boat and took a few steps. Then trouble appeared: "But when he saw that the wind was boisterous, he was afraid; and beginning to sink he cried out, saying, 'Lord, save me!'" (Matt. 14:30 NKJV). Jesus created the entire universe with a word. Certainly, He could have simply spoken and rescued the sinking Peter. In His dealings with people, however, He often chose to touch them. Matthew tells us, "And immediately Jesus stretched out His hand and caught him (v. 31 NKJV)."

On at least two occasions, Jesus provided for people by touching food. At one of these times, about twenty thousand people, including women and children, were listening to Him on a hillside. They were so enthralled by His message that they forgot to eat. Andrew found a boy who had the foresight to bring a sack lunch, the Happy Meal of that day, two little fish and some small barley loaves—more like biscuits. Jesus took the boy's lunch in His hands, said grace, and fed the whole crowd. John tells us, "Then those men, when they had seen the sign that Jesus did, said, 'This is truly the Prophet who is to come into the world'" (John 6:14 NKJV).

Each of these events demonstrates Jesus' willingness to encounter people in a very personal, powerful way. When He stood face-to-face on the shore with Legion, when the leper fell at His feet, when the woman wept because her only son was dead, when Jairus found out that his daughter was dead and Jesus' hopeful eyes met his, and a thousand other moments, Jesus didn't stand apart from them and give them advice. He touched them. That's what He did to me too. As I read the gospel accounts in Willie Lane's Bible study, it was as if I was standing in front of Jesus. In the New Testament accounts,

Jesus didn't stand apart from them and give them advice. He touched them.

He treated each person as though he or she was the only one in the world. That's how I felt. It wasn't just that "God so loved the world." It was that God loved *me*. I sensed Jesus' loving touch just as much as each of those people in the Gospels sensed it. And it changed my life.

THEY TOUCHED HIM

We often remember the woman in Luke's gospel who got down on the ground and reached through people's legs to touch the hem of Jesus' garment as He walked to Jairus's house. For a dozen years, she had suffered from internal bleeding. The doctors hadn't helped her even though she had spent all of her money on their services. She was desperate. Maybe she had heard about another time when, at the height of His popularity, people "sent out into all that surrounding region, brought to Him all who were sick, and begged Him that they might only touch the hem of His garment. And as many as touched it were made perfectly well" (Matt. 14:35–36 NKJV). In these cases, Jesus' power transformed the lives of people who had enough faith just to reach out to touch His clothes as He walked by. I think that's what happens every time our church feeds hungry people or invites people to worship with us. Many of them have just enough faith to walk in the door, but that's enough. They reach out and touch what they see, and God works in their lives.

Do you remember what happened when the bleeding woman touched Jesus' hem? He stopped. She had been healed, but that wasn't all that Jesus wanted. He used that moment to start a real relationship with her. Even though a crowd of people was there, and even though they were on their way to minister to a little girl in crisis, Jesus stopped to talk with this dear woman. His touch is not just for a moment. It may begin in an instant, but He wants to start a rich, real, vital relationship of give-and-take, loving and being loved.

AN INVITATION

I love Thomas, usually called "Doubting Thomas," because I'm so much like him. Many of us are. When Jesus told His men that they were going back to Jerusalem because His friend Lazarus had died, Thomas saw that as a problem—a big problem. The religious leaders had threatened to kill Him (and those who followed Him!), so he sarcastically muttered, "Great. Let's go with Him so we can die too."

His touch is not just for a moment. It may begin in an instant, but He wants to start a rich, real, vital relationship of give-and-take, loving and being loved.

After Jesus was raised from the tomb, He appeared to people on several occasions—but Thomas wasn't there. His friends excitedly told Thomas what they'd seen, but he didn't buy it. He told them, "Unless I see in His hands the print of the nails, and put my finger into the print of the nails, and put my hand into His side, I will not believe" (John 20:25 NKJV).

Thomas had been with Jesus for more than three years. He had seen thousands of healings, heard hundreds of messages, and looked into His eyes around countless campfires and on miles of dusty roads. It's easy to look at Thomas's doubts and conclude, "He should have known better. He should have believed like the others did. He's a bum!" But that wasn't Jesus' response. A week after Thomas's pronouncement of doubt, Jesus appeared to them again and gave a gracious invitation to His doubting friend. He told him, "Reach your finger here, and look at My hands; and reach your hand here, and put it into My side. Do not be unbelieving, but believing" (John 20:27 NKJV).

That did it for Thomas. He looked at Jesus and replied, "My Lord and my God!"(v. 28 NKJV).

I believe God gives us the same invitation today. The psalmist wrote, "Taste and see that the LORD is good" (Ps. 34:8 NIV). Our faith is based on sound reason, but it goes beyond our heads and into our hearts. We connect with Jesus by spiritual touch. Like the woman who reached between others' legs instead of walking up to Him, our faith may not be strong at first. Or, like Thomas, we may be very hesitant to believe God's love and forgiveness are real. God invites us to reach out to touch Him, and He delights in touching us.

LIKE ANDREW

Whenever we see Andrew in the New Testament, he's almost always bringing people to be touched by Jesus. That's our role today, to bring people to Jesus so He can heal their hurts, strengthen them in their weakness, and steady them in times of trouble. God has allowed us to touch a lot of people through St. John's, and it's a thrill to see it every time it happens.

Reginald Matthews was a New York Supreme Court Judge who was about eighty years old when he joined our church several years ago. He had lost his wife years before, and he missed her terribly. He told me that when he came to St. John's, he felt the love he had been missing since his wife died, and he wept every time he entered the building because he felt so deeply touched. Every time I talked to Judge Matthews, he would say, "Pastor Rudy, *this* is what church should really be like." He died on December 30, 2005, at eighty-eight years old.

A homeless lady who called herself "Neighbor" came to our church several years ago, and she attended every time the doors were open. She carried around everything she owned in a shopping cart, and she did a little covert panhandling at the services on Sunday mornings. I could tell a lot was going on in her mind, but she wasn't willing to open up. About two years after she first came to St. John's, I saw her and asked, "Hey, Neighbor. How are you today?"

She looked at me really hard and told me, "Pastor Rudy, my name is Carolyn. Don't call me 'Neighbor' anymore. You can call me Carolyn from now on." From that day, she has become deeply involved in the life of our church, especially our prayer ministry. People in our church cared for her, reached out and touched her, and her heart melted as she began to trust us. Not long after she told us her name had changed, she came forward to be baptized, and the whole church erupted in applause. It was a beautiful thing. Carolyn would tell you that God has surrounded her with people who accept her just as she is. They didn't try to fix her, they didn't demand that she get cleaned up, and they didn't expect her to respond quickly. They just kept loving her day after day, week after week, and they let her respond in her own good time.

Carolyn would tell you that God has surrounded her with people who accept her just as she is. They didn't try to fix her, they didn't demand that she get cleaned up, and they didn't expect her to respond quickly. They just kept loving her day after day, week after week, and they let her respond in her own good time.

Robert Williams was an alcoholic and drug addict, and when he first came to St. John's, he was homeless. Like other men living on the street, Robert felt isolated and marginalized. But also like so many other homeless people in Houston, God led Robert to our recovery ministry at St. John's, and a transformation began. God touched his life, he got sober, and soon he found a good job. After his life turned around, he met Marianne here at the church. They fell in love and got married. As Robert's recovery continued, he felt God leading him to help facilitate one of the recovery groups at our church.

As people watch Robert and Marianne, they are struck with his tenderness toward her. The tough, hopeless guy who lived on the street has become a strong, gentle husband, friend, and leader at St. John's. Today, they are two of the best representatives of God's great love here at St. John's, but as Robert would tell you, he's come a long way, baby!

Unconditional love isn't just good theology or church theory. It's our practice, and we are very intentional about it. We teach our people to make it a point to reach out to every single person who walks in the door. That means we get up and go sit next to people who might be addicts and those who wear thousand-dollar suits, those who are mentally ill and those who are rising in the corporate world, those who don't have a dime and those who gave a million dollars last year, those who smell like sewage and those who wear expensive cologne, those who are black and those who are yellow, white, or red. And we touch them.

Physically, we give people big hugs to express our unreserved love and acceptance for them. Sometimes I have to laugh at the response. Some white-collar folks are shocked when a homeless person takes the initiative to give them a squeeze. That's okay. They'll get used to it if they keep coming.

Physically, we give people big hugs to

express our unreserved love and acceptance for them. Sometimes I have to laugh at the response. Some white-collar folks are shocked when a homeless person takes the initiative to give them a squeeze. That's okay. They'll get used to it if they keep coming.

WHO IS MY NEIGHBOR?

One of the most famous parables Jesus told was the story of the good Samaritan. He was considered an outcast, a foreigner, and an unbeliever, but he reached out to help a man who had been robbed and beaten. And he didn't just speak a blessing and walk off. He carried the broken, bleeding man to town and paid for shelter and care until the wounds healed. He was involved, deeply and intentionally involved, in the life of the needy person.

God calls each of us to be a good Samaritan today. Who are the needy people around us? Let's correlate the types of people in Jesus' day to people in the inner city, the suburbs, and rural areas today.

• Poor people

Palestine was full of poor people. Most were farmers who were economically oppressed by unscrupulous tax collectors. The inner city today certainly has people who can identify with the poor people described in the Gospels. In every metropolitan area, tens of thousands are homeless, and many thousands more have shelter but live in poverty. It's a lot harder to find truly poor people in the suburbs, but some trailer parks contain people who live on food stamps. In the countryside, you can find pockets of people who are desperately poor, living at the level of subsistence, much like the inner-city poor and the people of Palestine.

• Lame and blind people

Beyond the physical handicap of disability, in Jesus' day these people experienced severe social and economic roadblocks. They were usually reduced to begging to get enough money to live another day. In the inner city today, millions of people are under-educated and untrained, stuck in a cycle of oppression. In the sub-urbs and rural areas, those on the fringe of society include those who don't speak English, and the elderly who are bypassed in our youth-worshipping culture.

• Lepers

In the time of the New Testament, lepers were the dregs of soci-ety. If they encountered people on the road, lepers were obligated to yell, "Unclean! Unclean!" to warn them to stay away. HIV-AIDS patients are the lepers of our age. Just a few years ago, people thought that any contact with infected people risked spreading the disease. In the suburbs and rural areas, sexually transmitted diseases are ruining the lives of millions of people. In addition, drug and alcohol addiction cause others to avoid them at all costs.

• The demon-possessed

Though I believe there are people today who are possessed or oppressed by demonic powers, mental illness is a modern, wide-spread parallel to the demon possession we find in the Gospels. An article published by the Treatment Advocacy Center of Arlington, Virginia, reveals a startling statistic about the number of homeless people who are mentally ill:

Approximately 200,000 individuals with schizophrenia or manic-depressive illness are homeless, constituting one-third of the approximately 600,000 homeless population (total homeless population statistic based on data from Department of Health and Human Services). These 200,000 individuals comprise more than the entire population of many U.S. cities, such as Hartford, Connecticut; Charleston, South Carolina; Reno, Nevada; Boise, Idaho; Scottsdale, Arizona; Orlando, Florida; Winston-Salem, North Carolina; Ann Arbor, Michigan; Abilene, Texas; or Topeka, Kansas.[3]

Looking at the problem from the other direction, about one in seven people who are mentally ill are homeless. A study by a research team at the University of California, San Diego School of Medicine, published in the *American Journal of Psychiatry*, found that 15 percent of those with serious mental illness are currently homeless. People suffering from schizophrenia, bipolar disorders, substance abuse, and those without publicly funded health care are most likely to be homeless. Men are more likely to be homeless than women, and blacks were more likely to be without permanent shelter than whites, Hispanics or Asians.[4]

Clinical depression is the primary form of mental illness that devastates suburbs and rural areas. The alarming increase in the use of antidepressant medications tells us that depression is an epidemic in these parts of our culture.

• *Tax collectors*

In the time of Christ, the Romans enlisted a few Jews to collect taxes from their countrymen. These tax collectors were considered traitors, and worse, they often extorted even more from chronically poor people. Understandably, other Jews despised them for betraying their people. In the inner city today, thugs, pimps and gangs use manipulation and intimidation to prey on their own people to make a buck. In the suburbs and rural areas, unscrupulous people in business take advantage of those they claim to serve.

• Samaritans

The power and surprise in Jesus' story of the good Samaritan was that someone who was ethnically despised came to the aid of a Jewish man in need. Samaritans were half-breeds, and their form of worship was unacceptable to Jews, so Jews avoided them if at all possible. In the inner city today, people feel threatened by violence, so they are suspicious of anybody who is different—socially, ethnically, financially, or in any other way. The population of the suburbs is relatively homogeneous. People have moved there precisely to avoid threatening contact, so anyone who is different is considered suspicious. Rural areas tend to be much more stable, with very little change in the ethnic or in religious mix of a community, a factor that often breeds intense suspicion of outsiders.

•Pharisees

The religious leaders of Jesus' day saw themselves as the keepers of the faith during Roman occupation. They jealously guarded the temple and their customs. They were the "enfranchised," the establishment. In the inner cities across the country today, we often find small groups of people who see themselves as the defenders of the city. They are sure they're right and everybody else is wrong. These same people can be found in the suburbs and rural areas. No matter where you go, you'll find a few people who think they know the answers to everybody else's questions and should be given the right to fix others' problems.

Who are "the least of these" in your world? If you can't identify them, you sure aren't going to touch them with love, understanding, and resources.

WHY NOT MORE?

Quite often, people look at our ministry and say, "Pastor Rudy, you're really different. You really love people, and the people at St. John's really love people too. Why don't more Christians love people that way?"

The answer I learned from Auntie Mae Mae is that most of us live in fear, not in love. We feel threatened because others are different from us, and we are self-absorbed, thinking about our own pleasures, our own comforts, our own possessions, our own safety, and our own prestige. *What would happen,* we wonder, *if I reached out to touch that person? What would people think of me? What if that person robbed me? What if he became dependent on me and took up too much of my time?* We're afraid that we'd lose something precious if we give of ourselves. Jesus saw this fear, and He spoke to it. He said, "Whoever desires to save his life will lose it, but whoever loses his life for My sake will find it" (Matt. 16:25 NKJV).

We can only express love, forgiveness, and acceptance if we've genuinely experienced them.

We can only *express* love, forgiveness, and acceptance if we've genuinely *experienced* them. Three passages remind us that we can't give away something we don't possess.

- John wrote, "In this is love, not that we loved God, but that He loved us and sent His Son to be the propitiation [satisfaction] for our sins. Beloved, if God so loved us, we also ought to love one another" (1 John 4:10–11 NKJV).

- Paul encouraged the believers in Ephesus, "Be kind to one another, tenderhearted, forgiving one another, even as God in Christ forgave you" (Eph. 4:32 NKJV).

- And Paul told the Roman Christians, "Accept one another, then, just as Christ accepted you, in order to bring praise to God" (Rom. 15:7 NIV).

We need to step back, take a good, hard look at our lives, and ask, *How much do I love the unlovely, forgive those who hurt me, and accept people who are different from me?* Your answer to that question tells you how deeply the grace of God has penetrated your own heart. If you and I have drunk deeply of God's love, forgiveness, and acceptance, they can't be contained. At the pinnacle moment of a feast in Jerusalem, Jesus stood up and cried out, "If anyone thirsts, let him come to Me and drink. He who believes in Me, as the Scripture has said, out of his heart will flow rivers of living water" (John 7:37–38 NKJV). The overflow of God's love, forgiveness, and acceptance will spill out of our hearts and into the lives of others: first, our families, then to every person we encounter every day. And we may even find that our love propels us to care for needy people who aren't in our paths each day. That's when we know our hearts are truly full and overflowing.

Rick Warren's best-selling book, *The Purpose Driven Life*, begins with a strong, clear statement: "It's not about you."[5] That's true. Our lives should be about God, not ourselves. We want to please God by following His will and fulfilling His purpose, but we come to that relationship as wounded, empty, sinful, and ashamed. At the beginning, we are desperate to be forgiven and to be filled with God's great grace. At the beginning, then, it's all about us. Only when we are filled and forgiven does our focus shift from necessary narcissism to altruism, from ourselves to God and others. The more we are filled and overflowing, the more we are thrilled with God's grace so that we delight in pleasing Him and helping others in need. Some of us are trying to overflow before our hearts have been filled. That just doesn't work.

Churches are a reflection of their leaders and their people, but make no mistake: a single person whose heart is aflame with the love of God can create a wildfire that spreads far and wide. We don't have to wait for a pastor or teacher or any other leader. We can start by ourselves today by responding to God's grace in our lives.

According to Robert Linthicum in his book, *Empowering the Poor*, ministries can be characterized by their attitude toward "the least of these." Some churches have ministries "to" needy communities, some minister "in" those communities, and some minister "with" needy people.

Ministering "to" needy people is keeping them at arm's length. A suburban church may take old clothes to a shelter and drop them off. They expect the effort will help in some way, but they have very little contact with homeless people or abused women and children served by the shelter. In some cases, though, ministering "to" is the best we can do. For example, tens of thousands of churches sent money to help victims of the tsunami in Indonesia, Thailand, India, and Sri Lanka. Thousands more assisted with relief in the aftermath of Hurricane Katrina that devastated New Orleans and other cities along the Gulf Coast. The vast majority of us can't go there to build relationships with those in need, so sending supplies and funds is the best we can do. In most cases, however, we need to move beyond ministering "to" a community to connecting "with" them.[6]

> *A single person whose heart is aflame with the love of God can create a wildfire that spreads far and wide.*

Many churches minister "in" their communities. The building is found in the town or city or countryside, but they see people outside the church as "them" instead of "us." They see their church as a haven from the injustice and heartache outside the church, and they develop a fortress mentality. If people come to them, the church will try to find them some help. But if they don't come, that's fine too.

In *Walking with the Poor*, Bryant Myers advocates "transformational development," which is the drive for a church to incorporate itself into the fiber of the community through relationships "with" people who live there.[7] Transformational development transcends the specifics of material and economic improvement and expands the effort to include the spiritual, emotional, social, and material empowerment of the whole person and the entire community. I believe God has called us to minister "with" a community, to get out into the fabric of people's lives and meet them where they are, to show the love of God in the midst of their joys and pain. Instead of the church being a fortress to protect us from threatening people, the church is a family that cares for all of its people, the saved and the lost, the rich and the poor, the clean and the smelly. Churches that minister "with" their communities live in love, not in fear.

A WARNING

There is tremendous power in touching people, figuratively or literally, but power can be abused. Human nature wants to control others, so be careful that your actions to touch others aren't tainted by a sinful desire to gain prestige or manipulate people in any way. Physical touch, especially cross gender, can be misleading. My policy is to never meet with a woman privately. I know that's a bit extreme, but it's my policy, and it works for my family, our church, and me. God has provided some wonderful women at St. John's to provide care for other women, and I'm glad to let them do what God has called them to do.

As you move forward in touching others with God's love, check your heart often. Don't be surprised if you find mixed motives and unhealthy desires. When you find them, turn to God, confess them, and repent. In the next chapter, we'll learn to see people the way Jesus saw them. That perception will help us keep our motives in line with God's purposes.

In his book *Just Like Jesus*, author and pastor Max Lucado observes that we learn from childhood that our hands have incredible power. He writes:

> Oh, the power of our hands. Leave them unmanaged and they become weapons; clawing for power, strangling for survival, seducing for pleasure. But manage them and our hands become instruments of grace—not just tools in the hands of God, but God's very hands. Surrender them and these five-fingered appendages become the hands of heaven.[8]

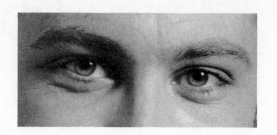

CHAPTER 4
Through His Eyes

But when He saw the multitudes, He was moved with compassion for them, because they were weary and scattered, like sheep having no shepherd. (MATTHEW 9:36 NKJV)

In short, Jesus moved the emphasis from God's holiness (exclusive) to God's mercy (inclusive). Instead of the message "no undesirables allowed," he proclaimed, "In God's kingdom there are no undesirables." —PHILIP YANCEY

Expectations are premeditated resentments. When we look at someone for the first time, we often form an opinion of that person's interior by looking only at his or her exterior. From the way she dresses, the way he walks, the way she laughs, the way he smells, the look in her eye, his topic of conversation, and a host of other external factors, we form an opinion of the person's character and conclude that this person is a threat, or not. In his latest book, *Blink*, Malcolm Gladwell observes, "The most common forms of *rapid cognition* are the judgments we make and the impressions we form of other people. Every waking minute that we are in someone's presence we are bombarded with a constant stream of predictions and interferences about what the person is thinking and feeling."[1] These expectations, born of ignorance, almost always result in disappointment or resentment— at least they have in my life. Fear is the root of these expectations. We're afraid that person—a family member or a stranger—will crack the shell of safety that we've carefully constructed to protect ourselves.

I try to encounter every person God brings across my path with an open mind and an open heart. For example, when I meet a person who is obviously wealthy or powerful, a corporate executive or a popular politician, I don't want to be distracted. I try to look past "bling-bling" and hyperdrive confidence to see into the person's heart. Before the lights came on for me and God changed my life, I would have expected that person to try to use me to get something he wanted, but I've realized that many wealthy or powerful people are genuinely compassionate. That surprised me. Now, I try not to make any assumption, especially a negative one. In the same way, before my epiphany about people, I assumed that homeless people weren't aware of how they looked, sounded, and smelled, and I assumed they were all illiterate. But getting to know many of them rocked my world and taught me that the veneer of dirt and old clothes often hides someone with a master's degree, or even a PhD, who is well aware of his or her appearance and smell.

In fact, our most commonly repeated statement at St. John's is, "I love you, and there's nothing you can do about it."

I used to approach people with a hidden agenda (often hidden even from me) that I needed people to respond in certain ways to meet my needs for safety and significance. But now, God has given me a new set of eyes, and I see them as people God loves, and I love them too. In fact, our most commonly repeated statement at St. John's is, "I love you, and there's nothing you can do about it." That comment is based on the perception that every person is valuable in God's eyes, and we want to love each one as He loves them. You see, loving people isn't about what they can do to meet my needs; it's about what God has done in my own heart to enable me to see them as He sees them.

THE JESUS THING

You never know how people will respond. Sometimes, when I give someone a hug or hold out my hand to shake his, a person gets tears in his eyes because he is melted by love. But on some occasions, I hold out my hand and people look at me as if I'm crazy (we call it "touched," which is another meaning of the word). At that moment, I could respond with resentment that my offer of love has been refused, or I can simply acknowledge the person's right to respond any way he chooses and know I've done what God wanted me to do. In that case, there's no anger, no resentment, and no fear—just a little more compassion for someone who, for some reason, can't receive love.

All I know is that at that point of contact, I've done the Jesus thing: loving people with a full heart and letting them respond any way they choose.

All I know is that at that point of contact, I've done the Jesus thing: loving people with a full heart and letting the individual respond any way he chooses.

When Jesus looked at people, He "was moved with compassion for them, because they were weary and scattered, like sheep having no shepherd" (Matt. 9:36 NKJV). How do sheep act when they feel alone and threatened? The word picture Jesus paints is of a flock of sheep "prostrated from exhaustion and neglect."[2] They look panicked, because they feel alone and helpless. Sooner or later, they give up in despair. That's what people do too. We shouldn't be surprised when people choose "fight or flight" as their reaction to difficulties. Both are responses to the nagging fear that their lives are out of control.

The question I'm addressing, though, isn't *their* fear—it's *our* fear. Until our own fears are cast out by God's great love for us, we'll continue to see every person as a stepping-stone to reaching our own selfish goals or a threat to our safety and significance. We'll see people as things, and we'll use them instead of loving them. The issue, then, is filling our own hearts with the incomparable love of God. That's the only way we can truly love other people. Then we can love them with no strings attached, without demanding certain responses to make us feel better about ourselves. Jesus communicated His love to many different people. I'm convinced He showed love to rigid, angry Pharisees just as much as He did to children and outcasts. One group delighted in His love; the other plotted to kill Him. But His love wasn't about premeditated expectations and anticipated responses. He was responding to the Father's will to show His love to every person, regardless of the response.

NEW EYES

When Paul met Jesus on the road to Damascus, his life was radically changed. As he got to know Christ better, Paul's perception of Him and of people radically changed too. In one of his letters to the people in Corinth, he wrote, "From now on we regard no one from a worldly point of view. Though we once regarded Christ in this way, we do so no longer" (2 Cor. 5:16 NIV). When Paul looked at Jesus "from a worldly point of view," he saw Him as a threat, and he went from city to city to capture and kill Christians. But after his encounter with Jesus, the scales literally fell from Paul's eyes, and God gave him a new perception of Jesus and the people around him. He no longer saw people, "from a worldly point of view." He now saw their hearts, and his new perception changed everything. That's what happened to me too.

In many ways and at many different times, Jesus explained what it means to follow Him. In a famous statement, He told us, "If anyone desires to come after Me, let him deny himself, and take up his cross and follow Me" (Matt. 16:24 NKJV). Denying ourselves doesn't mean we try to suppress our God-given personalities and abilities. Instead, it means we say no to sinful, selfish desires as we say yes to Jesus and follow Him. That's not something we do only once. I need to do it all day every day, because my selfishness has an unfortunate habit of rising up and trying to run my life again and again. If I

If I have to say no to my selfishness a hundred times a day, I'll do it.

have to say no to my selfishness a hundred times a day, I'll do it. But saying no is only half of the message. I also need to say yes to Christ: His kindness and His purposes.

In the same conversation, Jesus asked two penetrating questions: "For what profit is it to a man if he gains the whole world, and loses his own soul? Or what will a man give in exchange for his soul?" (v. 26 NKJV). Here's what I think these questions are getting at: Take the value of "the whole world"—all the gold, oil, real estate, diamonds, and everything else of value—and put it all on one side of a set of scales. On the other side, put the most obscure, poor "untouchable" from a slum in India. Jesus is saying that the value of that destitute person is far higher than all of the world's wealth! And that's the value of the person you sat next to at church last Sunday—and the person you avoided sitting next to. It's the worth of the powerful person you were afraid of last week—and the little boy with Down Syndrome you passed at the grocery store. It's the value of Beyoncé or Michael Jordan—and the incontinent old lady with Alzheimer's. That's the worth of your dearest friend—and the person from another culture you just don't understand. "Red and yellow, black and white, they are precious in His sight." All of them.

THE PURPOSE OF PAIN

We hate to hurt, but experiencing pain is a part of being human. The question is, how does pain shape our lives? For some of us, pain drives us "to the slab." That's the term homeless people use to describe life on the sidewalk or under a bridge. The excruciating pain of broken relationships and shattered dreams is too much for some of us to bear, and we give up hope.

It may take us a while to let God use pain in our lives for a good purpose, but if we'll let Him, He'll use it to knead our hearts like a lump of dough, and our hurts will drive us deeper into the grace of God. His love and His purposes aren't just *good things* to grasp; they are *absolute necessities* if we're going to survive. Sooner or later, God's Spirit brings us a new sense of hope—and a deeper, richer faith than we ever had before. And as our hearts fill with new hope, love, and joy, we can touch others in ways we never dreamed before. That's what happened to Paul.

If we could have seen Paul before Jesus met him on the road that day, I don't think many of us would have felt too comfortable with him. He was an angry, driven, powerful man. He had plenty of prestige, and he used his position to intimidate and control people. God took him through a long school of suffering to tenderize his heart and give him the ability to truly love others. His suffering wasn't anything Paul would ever have chosen, but he accepted it from the hand of God as his teacher. And his perspective about pain changed. He wrote, "If we are distressed, it is for your comfort and salvation; if we are comforted, it is for your comfort, which produces in you patient endurance " (2 Cor. 1:6 NIV). Did you get that? His distress helped him minister more effectively because he could identify with others' sufferings, and the comfort he experienced enabled him to pour out comfort to others who were hurting.

One of the most poignant moments in the gospel narratives is when Jesus met with Mary and Martha at the tomb of their brother, Lazarus. Jesus and His men had gone to another part of the country. His friend Lazarus became very ill, and the sisters sent someone to bring Jesus back to heal him. Jesus, though, delayed for a few days. In the meantime, Lazarus died and was buried in a tomb. When Jesus arrived, Martha, and then Mary, came out to confront Him with the painful fact that He hadn't come soon enough. As Jesus stood at the tomb of His friend, He was probably thinking of the loss of His good friend and the pain his death caused the sisters. The sting of death and disappointment touched His heart, and the Savior of the world bowed His head and wept.

Nothing could have comforted the sisters more at that moment. Their friend cared enough to weep for their brother. Even though Jesus was going to fix the problem by resuscitating Lazarus and re-storing him to life, at that moment by the tomb, He allowed Himself to feel His own pain and the pain of His friends. And He wept.

This account tells me something very significant about seeing people the way Jesus saw them. He identified with their pain. Yes, He had the answer to all of life's questions. Yes, He has the power to overcome any obstacle. But His first and primary connection with the sisters was to be touched by the same pain they experienced. And He wept.

My own pain has forced me to go deeper into the heart of God to experience His grace, truth, and strength in new ways. It hasn't been easy, but it's been necessary. Of course, my first purpose for dealing with it wasn't altruistic; I just wanted to find peace and hope again. But as I found God's comfort, I was able to empathize far more with others' wounds. Instead of resenting wounded, needy people for getting in the way of my goals, I was able to care for them. Instead of trying to feel good about myself by fixing their problems as quickly as possible (and taking the role of a Savior, though I hear that role is already taken), I can simply understand and comfort them where they are right now.

CONSISTENCY IS THE KEY

As we experience more of God's unconditional love—especially when we feel most unlovable—we'll be more secure. Then we won't see others as threats, and we'll be able to truly love them. As God works this out in our experience day in and day out, consistency is the key. When I first came to St. John's, a man who is mentally ill lived near the church. The first time I saw him, I extended my hand in friendship, and he growled at me. Yes, he growled! It was pretty easy to see him as a threat, and I was tempted to back away from him (who wouldn't?), but I conditioned myself to extend my hand and offer a warm smile every time I saw him.

At the other end of the social spectrum, sometimes I'm in an airport waiting for a flight, and I find myself sitting near a well-dressed executive. I've always had a certain relaxed look about me. I have a braided beard, and I wear jeans. Some people would say that I don't look much like a pastor. I only wear a suit and tie when one of the five Bs is happening: I'm *burying* somebody, I'm *borrowing* money, I'm *begging*, there's a *bride*, or I'm attending a *banquet*. Those are the only times. If you see me in a suit, I'm either going to one of those events, I'm already there, or I'm headed home. In the waiting area of the airport terminal, sometimes I catch an executive peering at me from behind his newspaper or looking over his laptop. He doesn't know what to make of that strange-looking guy! As he looks at me, he seems to be thinking, *You ought to know better.*

When I first came to St. John's, a man who is mentally ill lived near the church. The first time I saw him, I extended my hand in friendship, and he growled at me. Yes, he growled!

At those times, I have to look beyond a person's attitude and perception of me. Such people believe their opinion about life is the most important truth in the world—even their opinion *of me.* I could feel threatened by them and withdraw, or I could resent them and lash out at them. Or I can see them as people who are "weary and scattered, like sheep without a shepherd." Their arrogance is just their own way of acting out their sense of being threatened. I have a choice: I can react to their fear, or I can look beyond their fear and see into their hearts. They, like the man who growled, or my best friend, or anyone else, are valuable to God—and to me. (By the way, the growling man eventually mellowed and let me shake his hand each time we met.)

KEEPING SCORE

It's human nature to keep score in our relationships with people. We compare ourselves with others, and we want to know who's winning. Do I look better? Am I more respected? Do I make more money? And a thousand other stats can be analyzed in our mind's box score. We have an innate desire to win, to be on top, and be one up, and many of us try to accomplish this goal by putting others down. We look for any flaw we can find, and we focus on it ruthlessly. If we can assign blame to someone, we think we've moved up a notch. And to be honest, if we can assign enough blame, we think we can intimidate and control that person. We often use labels like "failure," "bum," "drunk," "crackhead," and a host of other negative words, to put others down in the hope of feeling better about ourselves. But God's Spirit is amazingly gentle. He never condemns so He can be one up. Blame kills love, and it works both ways: it makes us paranoid, because we're sure others are eager to blame us—and often they are!

One day, people came to Jesus and asked Him if some Jews who had been slaughtered by Pilate and their blood mingled with temple sacrifices were worse sinners than anybody else. If Jesus said yes, they could feel better about themselves. But Jesus refused to play the blame game. He said the people who suffered that awful fate weren't worse sinners at all. Then He told them, "But unless you repent you will all likewise perish!" (Luke 13:3 NKJV) Just to be sure they got the picture, Jesus recounted another tragedy when a tower fell and killed some people, and He repeated His conclusion: "Unless you repent you will all likewise perish!" (v. 5 NKJV).

The point isn't that everyone's blood will be mingled with sacrifices or that towers will fall on all of us. Jesus was saying two things: To begin with, it's pointless to compare one person's fate with others' and try to assign blame so that we can brag that we're better than them, because, of course, we're all in the same boat. All of us are sinners in the eyes of God, and all of us desperately need God's forgiveness. No one is superior; no one is exempt from blame. We all need to look into the darkness of our own hearts and be gripped with the reality of the depravity we find there. When we are convinced that we have received love and grace that we so richly *don't* deserve, we'll stop trying to affix blame so we can one up someone else. The experience of grace trumps blame and opens the door to loving others.

What do we see when we look at others around us? People are created in the image of God, but we have tarnished that image. We are fallen. The Bible doesn't mince words when it describes our character and condition. Apart from Christ, we are helpless and hopeless, enemies of God and alienated from Him. When we look at those we see every day, do we think they are unlucky to be in the shape they're in? Maybe. Perhaps they've had some hard knocks they don't deserve. That's part of

When we are convinced that we have received love and grace that we so richly don't *deserve, we'll stop trying to affix blame so we can be one up on someone else.*

living in a fallen world, and sometimes it's tragic. But there's a deeper issue: sin and separation from God. That's why Jesus said it's foolish to try to assign blame and keep score to be one up on someone else. Hard luck might evoke pity, but depravity and sin require the grace of God to forgive us and give us new life. That's the result of repentance, and that's what Jesus said everyone needs.

I don't ask why a person is homeless or jobless or cross-dresses or smells bad. I don't care if it's her fault, someone else is to blame, or if a meteor came from outer space and caused the problem. There's no need to assign blame, keep score, or label people. Instead, I just see someone Jesus is dying to love, someone who needs help, someone God has put in my path at the moment to touch in a tangible, meaningful way.

AT THE CENTER

Jesus was completely secure in the Father's love. He didn't need approval from people to feel good about Himself, so He was completely impartial in His relationships. He showed just as much love to Nicodemus, a powerful and respected Pharisee, as He showed to the shame-filled Samaritan woman who had had five husbands. He cared as much for the rich kid who couldn't part with his money as He did for the widow who put all she had into the offering plate. He didn't show preference for Jairus, the respected synagogue official, over the poor sick woman who touched His clothes. He didn't get worked up because one person got it and another didn't. He just loved them all. His goal wasn't to categorize them into believers and unbelievers, clean and unclean, righteous and unrighteous. He met each person where he was and tried to bring him to the center of God's presence so he could experience His love. As that happens, people's defenses go down and they begin to love each other. It's a beautiful thing.

His goal wasn't to categorize them into believers and unbelievers, clean and unclean, righteous and unrighteous. He met each person where he was and tried to bring him to the center of God's presence so he could experience His love.

It's not my job to make people love each other. I'd go crazy trying to do that. It's my role to try to bring people to the center of God's love so they can be transformed by His touch. Then God's fantastic love overflows and touches more people. But if it doesn't happen, I just keep nudging people to the center, pointing them on the path to Jesus. If they take a step toward Him, we all celebrate. If they don't, we don't get bent out of shape. It took me a long, long time to get it, so I can wait for other people to take their own time too.

ALL OF ME

When I see people the way Jesus saw them, and as I experience God's grace in my own life, love calls for *my whole being* to get involved in touching others' lives. Jesus gave all He had, and as I walk with Him, I learn to give all I have. Fear is the only thing that holds me back. As my fear is gradually washed away by God's love, I'll value others more than my security or selfish goals.

Building trust takes time, but honesty about my own pain and process tells [people] that I'm a safe person.

Giving all of me means I live in integrity in my relationships. I don't play games with people. I don't use them to advance my career or give me comfort and peace. People are inherently suspicious, but when they find that I'm not playing games with them, hiding my true motives, or manipulating them, they begin to trust me. Building trust takes time, but honesty about my own pain and process tells them that I'm a safe person.

Some people will read these paragraphs and conclude, "Rudy's nuts! There's no way I'm going to put all of myself into relationships. I've been hurt enough already." That's fine. Take your time. I believe all of us long to love and be loved. That deep desire eventually will propel many of us to identify obstacles in our path and cast them aside so we can experience and express more love than we ever imagined. Some of us, of course, will conclude that the risk is just too great, and we'll stay on the side of the road. I'm not asking anyone to conjure up a bunch of emotion or act in ways that don't fit your personality. I'm only saying that our perceptions about ourselves and other people will be changed by our encounter with Christ, and eventually, our experience of God's love will result in that love spilling out in some way into the lives of others.

When Jesus looked at people, He saw their need for God's love.

Some of them were aware of their need in the core of their beings, but some were clueless. He looked beyond their circumstances, and He looked past their appearance. He looked into their hearts, and He saw people who were afraid. Their fear might be revealed in timidity or defiance, being driven to succeed or collapsed in depression. Each one, though, needed to experience Jesus' touch. At St. John's, we've tried to capture that heart for others in a statement that we say all the time. I've already mentioned it in this chapter. We look at one another and say, "I love you, and there's nothing you can do about it." That's a statement of grace. (Sometimes when I lead people in saying this to each other, I tell them, "When you say that to the person sitting next to you, you might be lying right now, but it'll become real to you sooner or later.")

"THE CRASH"

"Compassion fatigue" isn't just a clever term. It's poison, and it's a danger for anyone who pours his or her live into others. Juanita and I both have experienced times when our bodies shut down and our souls were burned out.

On August 27, 1999, Juanita awakened to the usual routine in the Rasmus home. She started breakfast, and a minute or two later, she walked to the stairs and called out, "Girls, it's time to get up." She scurried back to the kitchen while she shouted, " Who wants juice? Anybody want milk instead?" Breakfast appeared on the table almost as soon as she announced it. (Watching Juanita in the early morning is like seeing a cross between a cook on a wagon train, ringing the bell for the cowhands, and a starting gun firing to start the runners at a track meet!) The second the girls and I got to the table, Juanita passed us en route to the shower. Before we had finished eating, she was out of the shower, dressed, and ready to go! Efficiency had always been her trademark: get it done, and get it done *right now!*

As Juanita reappeared, ready to go, I asked her, "Would you like me to take the girls to school this morning?"

She responded without a moment's hesitation, "Yes, that would be good. I don't feel too good."

Without warning, a horrible feeling suddenly had come over her. In some ways, it mimicked the flu, but she couldn't exactly describe what she was feeling. Also, she had no idea what the cause could be. In a few moments, she felt lightheaded, and her vision became blurred.

I hated to say anything, but her sickness didn't come at a very convenient time for me. I had a busy day planned, and her illness was raining on my little parade!

A few minutes later, Juanita was having trouble concentrating. She picked up the phone to call our church secretary to tell her that she would be late. She was thinking that if she could just lie down for a few minutes, she would probably be fine. Then it hit her, and she felt really awful. She told our assistant, "I won't be in today. No, *I won't be in at all.* Tell people I'm taking a leave of absence. No, no, tell them I'm taking a sabbatical. No, I'm taking a medical leave." And she hung up the phone.

Juanita went to the doctor, and his diagnosis was "clinical depression." We were shocked and confused, but we were determined to walk with God through this valley. For the next year, Juanita's days consisted of sleeping from eighteen to twenty hours each day. Depression isn't just "feeling blue"; it is emotionally, physically, and spiritually devastating. Juanita was consumed by the darkness that shut out the light in her life. She awakened each day to a new and deeper dread and a greater sense that she was falling into a dark pit.

Nothing, she was certain, could stop the downward spiral. After approximately three years of medical care, therapy, exercise, and prayer, she began to recover.

In our family, we call this time "the crash." In many ways, it shook our world to the core, but it also gave us the opportunity to learn some valuable lessons about ourselves, our family, and our ministry. Those lessons were learned in the crucible of pain, but today, they guide our lives in positive and powerful ways. Let me share what we learned:

- *We chose to be honest with the congregation.*

As soon as the doctor told Juanita that she had experienced a "major depressive episode," we told the church the truth. Far too often, pastors and their families in crisis pull down the shades and batten down the hatches to prevent anyone finding out they are struggling. We chose to do just the opposite. Deception wouldn't serve our congregation or us, so we told them the hard facts of our situation.

- *We allowed people to love us.*

Being honest with people made us vulnerable, but it also opened the door for them to express tender, strong love for us at a time when we were hurting. Telling people the truth honored them and built an even stronger bond of trust with them. In that spirit of trust and concern, their love poured out to our whole family. Truth is the foundation of a caring community. People often want to put their leaders on a pedestal, and some in our church thought Juanita and I should never struggle with problems like depression. Faith, though, doesn't insulate us from trouble; trust in God gives us strength and insight so that we can handle those troubles instead of being overwhelmed by them. When we were honest with people in our congregation, they knew we weren't superspiritual, untouchable, perfect Christians. We were human beings with the same hurts and hopes they experience. During those months and years, their care for our family had a powerful impact on the whole community. When we allowed them to show their care for us, their pastors, they could easily see themselves caring for everybody else in our community. God multiplied their love for us into love for thousands of others.

Truth is the foundation of a caring community.

- *We used "the crash" as an educational opportunity for our church.*

In many churches, mental health is a difficult issue. Many people don't understand mental illness at all, and some Christians believe every mental health problem can be explained as a struggle with demons. This event gave us the platform to inform people about the types of mental illness, especially the causes of depression, and the differences between diseases and demons.

- *Juanita and I learned to live in our present reality.*

In times of crisis, our minds tend to drift back to the way things *used to be* or to fast-forward to our hopes of how things *will be* in the future, when the pain is gone. "The crash" required Juanita and me to embrace our present reality with courage and discipline. Only then could we respond with *authenticity* by being ruthlessly honest about our emotions, being *attentive* to each other's fears and hopes, and making necessary *adjustments* in our lifestyle to fit the needs of the moment. For example, Juanita had always taken the girls to school every day. When she crashed, we had to make necessary adjustments in our roles, so I started taking the girls to school. Juanita had been a wonderful cook, but now it was my turn to provide our evening meals (mostly by eating out, because nobody wanted to eat my cooking!). During this time, I didn't travel as much, and I didn't accept as many speaking engagements. I needed to devote my energies to my family. Instead of wishing things were different and being angry about our present situation, we chose to respond to the actual, practical reality we faced each day. We were determined to be present with each other emotionally, spiritually, and physically.

• *We had a new urgency in our faith.*

The crucible of suffering clarifies our thinking and focuses our hearts, and pain exposes our dependence on God. A friend once told me, "We trust God as a last resort." "The crash" was the last resort for Juanita, the girls, and me, and we had to depend on God more than ever. During this time, we were desperate for God to give us wisdom, hope, and healing. We studied God's Word to find truths we could count on, and we prayed with more intensity than ever before. None of us would have chosen to go through this difficult time, but God used it to deepen our faith in Him.

• *God changed a lot of our "shoulds" to "wants."*

Before "the crash," Juanita and I certainly had been dedicated Christians. We wanted to serve God and please Him, but like many who serve God, some of our initial, pure zeal had gradually eroded, and some of our actions had become empty habits. We hadn't even recognized this shift in our hearts, but the crisis forced us to examine our motives. Now, instead of doing good things because others thought we should or because we felt we had to, God gave us a new vision, a fresh motivation, and a genuine desire to please Him by touching others' lives. Instead of ordering our lives just to please people around us or check off enough boxes on our to-do lists to keep from feeling guilty, we received a fresh, pure motivation to please God. Paul wrote about this pure motivation in his letter to the Colossians: "Whatever you do, work at it with all your heart, as working for the Lord, not for men, since you know that you will receive an inheritance from the Lord as a reward" (Col. 3:23–24 NIV). Before "the crash," our

Instead of ordering our lives just to please people around us or check off enough boxes on our to-do lists to keep from feeling guilty, God gave us a fresh, pure motivation to please Him.

attention was on what we were *doing* for God, but now we shifted our focus to *being* beloved, gifted, children of God. Then our doing would reflect our being.

• We had to admit our limitations.

In some ways, "the crash" occurred because Juanita and I were completely devoted to touching the lives of people in our community, and we had no sense of our limitations. Is it possible to care too much? Yes, if we feel responsible for every hurting, hungry, addicted, homeless, broken person we see, we'll burn out. Even Jesus took time away, hung out with His friends, and realized that the Father's will guided Him to specific people to be touched. Juanita and I had to learn that lesson too. Thousands of people in our community need to be touched, and many of them expect Juanita and me to touch them. Those expectations crushed us once, but we slowly realized that God is far bigger than two people, even two people who care deeply and are willing to expend their lives to touch those in need. As we walk as Jesus walked, our first priority is to enjoy our relationship with the Father, to draw deeply from His love, and then to trust Him to guide us to touch those He puts in our path. That's the only way to genuinely love so many needy people and stay sane.

Juanita's crash was a shocking, sobering, spiritual experience. In those long months, we realized we had been laboring under the crushing load of expectations—ours and others'—and we had lost touch with our own hearts, each other's needs, and the simplicity of our devotion to Christ. The school God took us through was incredibly difficult, but the lessons we learned changed our lives.

RECHARGE

Like Juanita, I've felt the need to recharge many times over the years. For me, one of the indicators that I'm on the edge (or over it) is when I have thoughts of quitting and finding something else to do. I've been faced with many challenges, some of which have made me question why I ever entered the field of ministry, but a good therapist, a nutritionist, and a trainer have been essential in my quest to continue serving the kingdom.

After I'd been the pastor at St. John's for a while, we were growing a lot, but I was getting tired under all the responsibilities. We decided to hire two consultants to give me some direction, and both of them told me that I was taking too much on myself. You might think I'd be happy to hear their advice, but I wasn't. I was frustrated and angry because they were suggesting that I give up some control. They wanted me to trust God and trust others by delegating more responsibility to them, and I simply didn't want to do it. I wanted people to see me as indispensable.

The freshness of loving people grew stale in the mundane mess of budgets and organizational charts. I was drying up spiritually and emotionally, and before long, I realized that I wasn't as effective as I had been, because I was operating in my own strength. In that moment, God gave me two messages: shift the burden of ministry from my shoulders to His, and connect more deeply with God's heart to find more love and strength than ever before. That was a turning point for me, and it has been a turning point for our ministry at St. John's too.

In that moment, God gave me two messages: shift the burden of ministry from my shoulders to His, and connect more deeply with God's heart to find more love and strength than ever before.

It's easy to get bogged down and overwhelmed by all the immediate, tangible, visible, tragic, consuming problems in people's lives. When the weight of all their problems—to say nothing of my own—gets too heavy for me, I can feel oppressed . . . hopeless . . . depressed. Regularly I need to refocus my heart on the infinite love and majesty of almighty God and let my heart fill with wonder. I have to move beyond the immediate to the transcendent so the love and the power of God can touch me again and again. This shift in focus is not an option for me.

I'm reminded of the story of the two-year-old girl who sneaks into the room of her newborn brother. Her parents watch and listen from a distance as she tiptoes up to the crib and whispers, "Quick, tell me what God looks like. I've almost forgotten." That's what happens to us too. When we first trust in Jesus, He is more real and alive than anything we've ever experienced. As responsibilities increase, however, we can lose that freshness and joy. Sometimes, like the little girl in the story, we need to hear from somebody who has "seen Jesus" more recently and is full of the thrill of that first encounter. It reminds us that Jesus' love is new every morning. In my life, the crush of responsibilities had moved me away from the most important things, and I felt wasted. But God brought some people into my life to remind me what Jesus is like, and I was refreshed again.

When we read the Gospels, we find that Jesus was intensely involved in people's lives, but He often took time alone or with His disciples to retreat, regroup, and recharge. That's not a sign of weakness. It's a necessity if we're going to stay involved in the nitty-gritty details of people's lives and give all of ourselves to them. I love people. I really do. But I can't keep loving people if my spiritual and emotional tank is empty. The overflow can only continue if I keep drinking deeply of God's love for me. For that to happen, I have to get away so I can be quiet and hear the whisper of God's Spirit.

In his book, *Margin*, Dr. Richard Swenson observes that the vast majority of us live on the edge of exhaustion. Our lives are filled with many demands. Without shock absorbers of quiet and reflection, even a minor setback can devastate us. Swenson argues persuasively that we need to intentionally create daily times of quiet and reflection, as well as more extended times of relaxation, study, interaction, and laughter to absorb the shocks of our bumpy lives.[3] These times are essential to refresh us and prevent burnout. Juanita has taught me a lot about the need to recharge my spiritual batteries. Dealing with her own pain has taught her that she has to stay intimately connected to the Source of love and light, so she follows some time-tested practices to focus her heart on the rich love of Jesus.

Christ often took time alone to pray. Sometimes He prayed all night; sometimes He got up early in the morning to pray. Whatever it took, He was committed to staying connected to the Father and the Father's will. But the toll of caring for others caused Him to take His men and get away for a few days from time to time. Extended time of prayer, encouragement, study, relaxation, and a few laughs revive tired spirits. "Compassion fatigue" is a threat to anyone who cares for people, and giving all we've got to anyone who comes into our lives makes us vulnerable to exhaustion.

If we're committed to following the example of Christ in compassion for needy people, we should also follow His example in recharging our souls daily and on retreats. That's not optional. It's standard equipment for a life of love. Burnout is inevitable if we try to keep going when our spiritual and emotional batteries are dead.

I could tell hundreds of stories about God using people in our church to touch people's lives. Love has the power to transform, to motivate, and to heal, but it's God's love that changes people, not manufactured love. We can't create that kind of love on our own. We'll burn out and give up, and we'll resent people instead of caring for them. It has to be a God thing.

A TOUCHING STORY: AMBER DAVID

At the age of thirty-five, Amber David finally learned to be a man.

Childhood incest and abuse had robbed him of his confidence and masculinity. Relatives had sexually abused him because he was effeminate. Other family members thought they could make him "more manly" by beating him.

He told me, "Because of the incest I experienced, I hated myself when I was a child, and I wanted to die. When I was eleven, I planned to commit suicide. My family had told me that all children under twelve went to heaven if they died, so

I wanted to kill myself before my next birthday. But God stopped me. That's the only explanation for it. God stopped me because He had a bigger plan for my life."

To deal with the pain, Amber became an addict. But once again, God stepped in, and in a wonderful twist of fate, Amber got sober at the drug rehab center that used to be our motel! Around that same time he discovered he was HIV positive. In rehab, someone told him about St. John's, so he came to check us out.

Amber had lots of questions. Like a lot of people, he was very suspicious of church and of Christians. I met with him soon after he began attending with us, and we talked about faith, Jesus, God's will, and a host of other issues. He always introduced his questions by saying, "Pastor Rudy, I want to get this right." But it wasn't just that he wanted right answers about God; he wanted to find people he could trust. Understandably, it was very hard for Amber to trust *anyone*—especially anyone in a position of authority. He told me, "It takes a village to raise a child, but you better be sure who's in the village!"

When Amber had been at St. John's for a while, he was clean and sober, but he was still struggling with his anger, his self-pity, and his sense of manhood. The wounds caused by incest and abuse do not heal easily. He told a friend, "I saw myself as damaged goods. I wasn't worthy to be loved by anybody, and I hated other African-American men. But as I spent time with Rudy and Juanita, I saw a healthy, loving marriage and a man who was comfortable with his manhood. As I hung out with them, I was liberated. I learned to be a man, and I accepted my manhood as a gift from God."

I talked to Amber about turning his pain into a platform

for helping others. Yes, he was wounded, but he could become a "wounded healer." I asked Amber to give his testimony at church in all three services. As he thought and prayed about what he would say, he felt God telling him to stand before the church "naked and unashamed." And that's what he did. He told the truth—the whole truth—about his pain and God's forgiveness and healing.

Amber tells people that being raised as a child of God at St. John's has been a life-changing experience. But it was his courage to help others that opened the door for an incredible ministry to men and women in our community.

CHAPTER 5
Holy Disgust

"Woe to you, scribes and Pharisees, hypocrites! For you are like whitewashed tombs which indeed appear beautiful outwardly, but inside are full of dead men's bones and all uncleanness. . . . Serpents, brood of vipers! How can you escape the condemnation of hell?" (MATTHEW 23:27, 33 NKJV)

What we meet in the biting language of Christ is a form of love that corresponds with the real world of corruption and the dullness of our hearts and the magnitude of what is at stake in our choices. —JOHN PIPER

The stained-glass dude just won't do. That image doesn't represent the passionate Jesus I see in the Gospels. When we take Jesus out of the windowpanes, we find a man of tender love and harsh words. Both. Not one or the other. But don't misunderstand: His harshness wasn't like ours. Our harsh words are most often spoken because we feel threatened, but Jesus wasn't worried about losing anyone's approval. He was completely, absolutely secure in the Father's love.

His love for people spilled out in tenderness, and it also surfaced in holy disgust against injustice. Genuine love demands an impassioned defense of the helpless and a struggle against oppression.

Auntie Mae Mae is the best human example of this blend I've ever seen. She was as tender and attentive as a mother with a newborn as she related to every person who came into her store, but she was passionate and assertive to correct injustice when she found it. She defended the hurting and the helpless against anyone who abused them. Her disgust produced an anger that was different from any I'd ever seen. She was never out of control, she never lashed out in rage, and she never crossed the line of saying too much too harshly. But make no mistake about it; she was crystal clear. Nobody had to wonder what she meant. Auntie Mae Mae spoke the truth with the hope that the person would repent, not just to vent her rage and assign blame.

JESUS' EXAMPLE

In his excellent little book, *Seeing and Savoring Jesus Christ,* John Piper observes:

We have seen the sweetness of [Christ's] mercies and how patient and kind and forgiving he was. That is why his severe speech cannot be written off as peevishness or as flares of temper or callous hostility. . . . If there were no great evils and no deaf hearts and no eternal consequences, perhaps the only fitting forms of love would be a soft touch and tender words. But such a world does not kill the Son of God and hate his disciples. There is no such world.[1]

One of the best-known moments of Jesus' holy disgust was when He "cleansed the temple." More than anything in the world, Jesus wanted people to experience the love and strength of God. When He came to the temple, though, worship of God was being distorted by people who wanted to profit from selling animals for sacrifices and exchanging Roman coins for ones accepted as offerings in the temple. John tells us, "And He found in the temple those who sold oxen and sheep and doves, and the moneychangers doing business. When He had made a whip of cords, He drove them all out of the temple . . . and poured out the changers' money and overturned the tables" (John 2:14–15 NKJV).

Today, you and I may be astonished that the "Lamb of God" would act so boldly, but I'm quite sure the people in the temple that day were even more surprised by His actions. But notice that His behavior wasn't a fit of rage. John tells us, "He made a whip of cords." That took time. Jesus saw the situation, stepped back, and prepared to take bold action. Part of His preparation was to get some strips of leather and patiently construct a whip to use when He made His statement of holy disgust.

IN MY WORLD

When we watch the evening news, we see injustice in almost every story: people in North Korea are starving because their dictator uses the nation's resources to build up his military might; a corporate executive's greed has led him to steal millions from shareholders; a thief murders a husband and wife and steals their possessions. The tragedies on the continent of Africa are mind-boggling: In several countries, up to 40 percent of the adults are infected with HIV-AIDS. In the civil war in the Darfur region of the Sudan, it is estimated that three hundred thousand people have died. Drought in Ethiopia and the surrounding nations has killed a million people. These statistics, though, don't show us the faces of millions of children left alone, destitute, and hopeless because their parents have died from disease, drought, and war. And particularly appalling are the "child soldiers" of Liberia, who fight for the insurgents against the government. These boys, some as young as six years old, carry rifles and machine guns. They are witnesses of—and sometimes participants in—murder, rape, and torture.

The injustices we see every day may not make the headlines, but they are real and immediate.

We see so many stories like this on the news that it's easy to be overwhelmed and become numb to them all, but it's important to avoid becoming calloused to injustice in our own world. The injustices we see every day may not make the headlines, but they are real and immediate. We can (and should) do something about them. In our community every day, I see battered women and abused children, employers who don't treat their employees fairly, and people who take advantage of anybody who drops his guard for an instant. If I just shake my head and walk away, I'm abdicating my responsibility as an ambassador of Jesus Christ. The prophet Micah outlined our responsibility very clearly. He wrote, "He has shown you, O man, what is good; and what does the LORD require of you but to do justly, to love mercy, and to walk humbly with your God?" (Mic. 6:8 NKJV)

When we "love mercy," we will sometimes be called upon to act boldly in "doing justly." It's a package deal. Most of us are wary of taking bold stands, because we don't trust our anger to be a form of holy disgust. To be honest, there's every reason to have that hesitation. The vast majority of anger and defiance that we see—in others and in ourselves—isn't holy at all. The goal of these emotions isn't justice and restoration; it's revenge. When the Holy Spirit taps us on the shoulder and shows us this wrong motive, we need to confess it as sin and repent. Let's be clear: The *emotion* of anger isn't sin, but the *actions* of anger can be sinful or righteous. Paul encouraged us to "be angry and do not sin" (Eph. 4:26 NKJV). If the emotion of anger is channeled in proper, productive ways, it can be a powerful fuel for good.

> *If the emotion of anger is channeled in proper, productive ways, it can be a powerful fuel for good.*

In many cases, change doesn't occur unless and until anger propels someone to take action—on a national level, like the Civil Rights Movement; on a local level, like housing ordinances that provide low-cost shelter for poor people, and on a personal level, when we "stand in the gap" to defend an abused or neglected friend against injustice. Complacency isn't a fruit of the Spirit, and passivity and fear aren't products of a life of faith. Holy disgust crystallizes our thinking and propels us to action.

TOXIC RELIGION

Jesus said some pretty demanding things to His followers. He told them that our love for Him must surpass our affection for every other person in our lives, even our family members. He said, "He who loves father or mother more than Me is not worthy of Me. And he who loves son or daughter more than Me is not worthy of me" (Matt. 10:37 NKJV). In Luke's account, Jesus took it a step farther: "If anyone comes to Me and does not hate his father and mother, wife and children, brothers and sisters, yes, and his own life also, he cannot be My disciple" (Luke 14:26 NKJV). He said His way is narrow and hard, and He told them that those who followed Him shouldn't look back in regret over what they'd left behind.

All of these statements were both an invitation and a warning: "Come follow Me, but count the cost of discipleship." Jesus wasn't advocating that people actually despise their family members. Instead, I believe He wants each of us to love Him so much that nothing and no one else can dislodge Him from the center of our affections. Actually, as we love Him with all our hearts, we'll love people with a love that has been refined by the fire of His purity and grace. Christ's warm invitation to His followers included the warning that following Him would require everything in us.

I appreciate Lord Acton's statement, but I'd put it a little differently: pastorin' ain't pimpin'.

His tone was much different, however, when He spoke to the religious leaders whose multiplied rules and quest for power prevented people from experiencing God's grace. Jesus called them "whitewashed tombs": pretty on the outside but dead on the inside. Their influence was so toxic that He called them "vipers," poisonous snakes. They were purveyors of toxic religion.

As British Lord Acton famously stated, "Power corrupts, and absolute power corrupts absolutely." Religious power has just as much capacity for corruption and evil as political or military might—maybe more because it almost always wears the mask of trustworthiness.

I appreciate Lord Acton's statement, but I'd put it a little differently: pastorin' ain't pimpin'. Pimps use people for riches and power. They wear fancy clothes and drive nice cars, but their wealth is acquired by the abuse of power. When their girls don't bring in enough cash, pimps beat them. Pimps use promises and intimidation to get girls to be loyal and bring in revenues. They promise to take care of them and make them look pretty, but there's always a threat hanging over their heads. This double message—promises and threats—is incredibly controlling and manipulative. This may sound harsh, but I sometimes see the same pattern at work in some churches. I get upset when the city government passes policies that aren't helpful to poor people, but I experience genuine holy disgust when I hear of pastors who are using their positions of authority to "pimp" their people. These leaders are much like the Pharisees and Sadducees of the Gospels, enjoying wealth and power at the expense of others. I hear pastors misrepresenting God by promising that if their people will give generously to the church, God will make these people rich. And I see pastors acting like kings of Third World countries, expecting everybody to bow to them and obey their slightest request.

I have to ask myself, *Why do people follow church leaders like this?* I believe they follow them for the same reasons people followed the religious leaders in Jesus' day, and prostitutes follow pimps today: fear, guilt, and greed. We are naturally in awe of powerful people, and we assume that they achieved power because they've earned it. Or maybe we've seen what happens when someone questions the motives or actions of these leaders. At one point, Jesus healed a blind man, and the Pharisees questioned him about the event. When he didn't give them the answer they wanted to hear, they kicked him out of the temple. For him, and for some of us, crossing religious authorities can lead to being ostracized. But for many of us, fear drives our decisions. It's much safer to get along by going along, keep the blinders over our eyes, and avoid making waves. And we keep going along to avoid the guilt and blame we'd suffer if we said, "Enough is enough!"

But another factor keeps us locked into toxic religion: when powerful people promise we'll get wealthy and healthy by following their directions. We don't want to be left out. We want all we can get, so we believe their promises, and we do whatever they tell us to do. When some extra money unexpectedly comes our way, we confirm that the pastor's promises are true. When our health or finances plunge, however, we keep quiet, because we sure don't want anybody to know it didn't work for us. After all, we're convinced it works for everybody else!

I have to ask myself, Why do people follow church leaders like this? *I believe they follow them for the same reasons people followed the religious leaders in Jesus' day, and prostitutes follow pimps today: fear, guilt, and greed.*

This thirst for power and the lack of integrity is what led my father to conclude, "You can't trust preachers and church folk." But now I'm one of them, and I'm well aware that my heart is just as dark as anyone else's. I'm just as capable of pimping people around me, and it scares me to death that I could become a person my father warned people about. Most fear is destructive, but this one is tremendously beneficial. I never promise that people will get rich if they give to our ministry. I tell them they should give out of a relationship, not as leverage to get wealthy. The purest motive to give is because we appreciate God's love. In any relationship, we give and receive. In our relationship with God, we receive a lot and give back only a little. We have received forgiveness, freedom, peace, purpose, and life. In response, we want to assist His work. I tell people that if they can't see God's work happening at St. John's, they should just put their money back in their pockets and keep it. If they don't think our ministry is worth supporting, we don't want it. But if they can see the results of God's Spirit at work in and through us, and if they want to respond to God's grace in their own lives, they can give as much as they want.

They're not giving to Rudy Rasmus—they're giving to God and to God's work to touch more lives for Jesus' sake. No promises of riches . . . just the joy of being a part of God's work. It's as simple as that. In a pimpin' environment, only the pimp prospers. But in a place where God and God's work are honored, everyone prospers.

THE COST OF CARING

In an alarming statement, Jesus warned, "Do not think that I came to bring peace on earth. I did not come to bring peace but a sword" (Matt. 10:34 NKJV). Wasn't He called "the Prince of Peace"? Don't we know Him as "the Lamb of God"? Yes, but He is also "the Lion of Judah," a God of power and purity, of strength and justice. As we follow Him, we'll learn to care about the things He cares about: love—the tenderness of grace and fairness—the hard reality of truth. Following Jesus in a life of holy disgust comes at a price.

> I tell people that if they can't see God's work happening at St. John's, they should just put their money back in their pockets and keep it. If they don't think our ministry is worth supporting, we don't want it.

If you value a neat, clean, safe life, don't get involved in defending people against injustice. It's messy, often disappointing, and requires tremendous tenacity to keep fighting against the forces of oppression. And they fight dirty. Like Jesus, you can expect to be criticized by your enemies and misunderstood by your friends. Those you are trying so hard to help can become impatient and wonder why you aren't making life better, faster, for them.

As our hearts become inflamed with the light of God's truth and grace, we'll find that some—perhaps many—of the things we once treasured aren't so valuable anymore. Malcolm Gladwell observes that our preoccupation with the acquisition of things is our primary faith challenge, because it steals our hearts away from God and isolates us from people in need.[2] No matter how much we have, it's not good enough. We may get a new house or car or pretty dress or electronic gadget, and we enjoy it for a while. But soon we notice that somebody else has a nicer one or a newer one, and the fire of desire burns hot. It's hard to be committed to God's purpose, God's plan, and God's promise when they don't include a fifty-inch plasma television set with the latest audio equipment. The major challenge of the enfranchised, the well to do, is facing the reality that God's purposes and priorities might be a little different from their own. They are happy to follow Christ as long as He doesn't ask for more than they are comfortable giving. But if anything close to real sacrifice is required, many are quick to bail out. A life of holy disgust requires a heart riveted on Jesus and holding our possessions with an open hand. "It is hard," Jesus said, "for a rich man to enter the kingdom of heaven" (Matt. 19:23 NIV).

A life of holy disgust requires a heart riveted on Jesus and holding our possessions with an open hand.

Riches promise safety and comfort, but they result in isolation and spiritual numbness. That's too high a price to pay for a few more things in this life, and it's a terribly high price to pay when we stand before Jesus to give an account of what we valued here on earth.

Exposure to the needs of people challenges the enfranchised. It challenges their time and their pocketbooks, but far more, it challenges their hearts. They have to decide if they will retreat into safety again, or if they will reassess everything about their lives and channel their resources according to God's leading. One Sunday a couple of weeks after Hurricane Katrina caused an influx of New Orleans residents to Houston, I felt compelled to explain why I wear blue jeans and a baseball cap when I'm preaching. (I actually give this explanation periodically for the benefit of new members and visitors.) My talk that morning included an update on my recovery from the cussing habit my father passed on to me (384 days and counting!). As soon as my update was finished, a well-dressed family from New Orleans, sitting near the front of the church, got up and left. Was it something I said? I would have thought they'd be impressed that I've stopped cussing!

We've had dozens, maybe hundreds, of well-dressed people come to St. John's, but most of them came only one time. They look around, and they feel uncomfortable with the needy people they see sitting next to them in the pew. At that moment, they have a decision to make. The question may not be formulated in a crystal clear way in their thinking, but it's instinctive: *Do I want to stay here and be a part of a gut-level, caring community, or do I want to go down the street to a church where people look, smell, and sound more like me?*

OPPORTUNITIES NEXT DOOR

Many church leaders report that mission trips by their members change lives. They go to East Africa, Indonesia, Guatemala, Mexico, and many other poor places around the world to build houses and churches. Observers report, though, that the most significant change occurs in the hearts of *those who go*, not the ones who are *the recipients* of their efforts. Many of these Americans have never been exposed to abject poverty, hunger, and disease. Seeing these people in a foreign land, up close, and touching them in a personal way shocks their souls more than a thousand sermons ever could. Many of them come back with a renewed commitment to make their lives count for Christ. They become devoted to caring for the oppressed and rectifying injustice. If their home churches will keep the flame burning, incredible things can happen.

But Americans don't need to spend thousands of dollars and travel around the globe to find people who are poor and oppressed. I see them every day. Just come to St. John's. We'll connect you with plenty of people for you to care for. I appreciate what Bono has done to raise awareness about the need for HIV-AIDS prevention and treatment in Africa. His holy disgust prompted him to become an activist for them, but I don't have to go to Africa to find those people. Half of the children in our school are HIV positive. Seeing them inflames holy disgust in me—not *about* them, but *for* them—and I am compelled to take action to help them.

Americans don't need to spend thousands of dollars and travel around the globe to find people who are poor and oppressed. I see them every day.

In the suburbs, people don't rub shoulders with truly poor people. Suburbanites go to their grocery stores, and they wonder which type of dinner they'll prepare tonight. But in some parts of the city, the question is not *which type* of food to eat, but *if* they'll eat tonight. For the poor, abject need is a daily reality, not a sociological theory.

If you come to our church, you'll shed tears of pain, feel holy disgust at injustice, and sense the transforming power of God's grace. Does that sound like something you're interested in?

I'm filled with holy disgust when I see big churches building even bigger buildings while their people drive their nice cars through poverty-stricken neighborhoods to get to church. They sing and praise God in their multimillion-dollar sanctuary and provide all kinds of wonderful programs for their middle- and upper-class members, but the leaders of these churches don't even make their members aware of the desperate needs all around them.

In spite of what we've heard in the news about the growing economy, fifteen thousand men and women will sleep outside in Houston tonight because they don't have anywhere to stay. Many thousands more would be out there with them, but a relative or a friend will give them a place to sleep tonight. As I write these words, people are lining up to receive a handout of a meal because they don't have a place to cook or don't have money to buy food. Thousands of little children have assumed adult responsibilities just to survive. A parallel world exists out there—not far from your neighborhood—and it's desperate for help. They need more than empathy. They need someone to step into their lives and provide some resources. Jesus didn't see people as sheep without a shepherd and only worry about them. He moved among them, touching them, listening to them, and connecting with them personally. That's how they knew He cared.

Most people in America are intentionally isolated from those who live in poverty, disease, and mental illness.

Some who read this book know exactly what I'm talking about because they're on streets and in the projects with people. But most people in America are intentionally isolated from those who live in poverty, disease, and mental illness. I'm not sure which comes first, the caring or the touching, but both are essential. If this chapter has moved you to care, by all means take action to touch a person in need. But if you still haven't connected emotionally with others' needs, take the initiative to go to them, to be with them, to see and hear for yourself what their lives are like. When you do, a sense of holy disgust will fill your soul, and you won't be able to stand it until you help them.

If we stay in the fight, the rewards of seeing lives changed are worth it. I've seen people who had no hope who now have a sense of freedom and purpose. Those who felt only loneliness and hurt now know they are connected to people who love them. Those who had nowhere to go now have a place to call home. But beyond the joy we see in each of these faces, we sense the smile of God—and that means everything.

If we stay in the fight, the rewards of seeing lives changed are worth it.

One person who is moved by holy disgust can change a lot of lives, but when several people band together, amazing things can happen. The Civil Rights Movement languished for many years after the Fourteenth Amendment was passed. Decades later, on December 1, 1955, in Montgomery, Alabama, Rosa Parks refused to give up her seat to a white man on a bus. When she was arrested, the black community boycotted the bus system for more than a year. Dr. Martin Luther King's support of the boycott was instrumental in leading the successful boycott.[3] This initial success was the spark that ignited the modern Civil Rights Movement and changed the shape of American life. Dr. King later observed:

We have the power to change America and give a kind of new reality to the religion of Jesus Christ. And we can get those young men and women who've lost faith in the church to see that Jesus was a serious man precisely because He dealt with the tang of the human amid the glow of the Divine and that he was concerned about their problems. . . . [Jesus was] the greatest revolutionary that history has ever known. And when people tell us when we stand up that we got our inspiration from this or that, go back and let them know where we got our inspiration.[4]

CHAPTER 6
Walk This Way

He who says he abides in Him ought himself also to walk just as He walked. (1 JOHN 2:6 NKJV)

For many of us the great danger is not that we will renounce our faith. It is that we will become so distracted and rushed and preoccupied that we will settle for a mediocre version of it. —JOHN ORTBERG

In most books on Christian living and discipleship, authors tell us our goal is to "become like Christ," or to "be conformed to the image of Christ." They then often list the "fruit of the Spirit" in Paul's letter to the Galatians (love, joy, peace, patience, etc.) as qualities God wants to produce in us. That's good. I'm cool with that. But at the risk of admitting I'm a bit of a heretic, I have to confess that this kind of terminology sounds kind of sterile . . . antiseptic . . . bland to me. When I look at the life of Jesus in the Gospels, I see anything but a sterile life. He was edgy!

WHAT DOES THAT MEAN?

I like the way John described it in his first letter. He said that if we say we are really following Jesus, we will "walk just as He walked." What in the world does that mean? Here's my list of what I think it means (you may have your own list):

- Jesus didn't use love as leverage. He didn't love people to get them to change. He just loved them and let them respond. Some of them repented and found love and hope; some hated Him and plotted to kill Him.

- He didn't own much (a tunic, sandals, and maybe some lip balm), and He never seemed to care about acquiring things. In fact, He was really wary about the destructive power of things. Freedom and joy seemed to come from giving stuff away.

- He loved people and used a few rules—not the other way around.

- Jesus regularly hung out with riffraff, sick folks, prostitutes, and other outcasts.

- He wasn't afraid of powerful, rigid people.

- He asked really hard questions, and when people asked Him questions, He didn't give simple answers—if He gave any answers at all.

- He loved people so much that He was severely criticized for it.

- At least once or twice, He used calculated violence to make a point. (I probably shouldn't have included this one, but it's the truth. Maybe protesting is the same thing for us.)

- He was rigidly nonpolitical ("Render to Caesar . . .")

- He taught and modeled a powerful combination of truth and grace.

- He accepted everybody, but He never abandoned the brutal truth to accommodate differences.

- As almighty God in human flesh, Jesus was infinitely superior, but common people felt completely comfortable with Him because He loved them without patronizing them.

- Rigid, self-righteous, power-hungry, political people felt threatened by Him and hated Him.

- He prayed often, long, and hard.

- He had such a clear sense of His purpose and strong trust in the Father that He was never in a hurry, even though the weight of the world was on His shoulders.

- Popularity and success never went to His head. He always moved toward people in need, not toward people who would give Him applause and power.

- Interruptions (like four guys lowering a paralyzed friend through the ceiling in the middle of His talk) never fazed Him. He saw every moment as an opportunity to do the Father's will.

After looking at how Jesus related to the Father and to people, it's easy to see that He was quite different from anyone else who ever lived. If God's direction to me is to "walk just as He walked," I have to ask myself, *how much am I really walking like Jesus?* And I'll ask you the same question: *How much are you walking like Jesus?*

ATTITUDE, ACTIVISM, AND AUTHORITY

James wrote, "Faith without works is dead" (James 2:17). In a similar way, empathy without activity is worthless. When I'm hurting, it doesn't help me very much for someone to stand in the distance and tell me he's sorry for me. I need someone to step into my world, recognize my need, and take steps to meet it. That's what real love does.

I want to turn from looking at Jesus to examining someone—someone like you and me—who was committed to walking with God and being radically transformed by His love: the apostle Paul. His letter to the Philippians contains one of the clearest descriptions of a life of faith found anywhere in the Bible. In the first few verses of the second chapter, Paul tells us that a life of faith is a response to the wealth of comfort, love, intimacy, and grace God has poured out on us. Because Christ's grace has been lavished on us and has filled our hearts to overflowing, we can take our eyes off ourselves and has put them on the needs of others. In the following verses, Paul outlines the *attitude, activism,* and *authority* of a life that pleases God. Let's look at those.

•Attitude

To make his point clear, Paul points us to Jesus as our model. He says, "Your attitude should be the same as that of Christ Jesus" (Phil. 2:5 NIV). What was Jesus' attitude? He was completely, absolutely, totally enamored with the Father's love and abandoned to the Father's will. Before His incarnation, Jesus simply spoke, and the entire universe came into being. He didn't even have to sweat! He is the awesome King and Creator, but "He humbled Himself and became obedient to the point of death, even the death of the cross" (v. 8 NKJV). Amazingly, the almighty God is also a humble

Servant. Augustine marveled at the paradox of the incarnation. He wrote:

> Man's maker was made man that He, Ruler of the stars, might nurse at His mother's breast; that the Bread might hunger, the Fountain thirst, the Light sleep, the Way be tired on His journey; that Truth might be accused by false witnesses, the Teacher be beaten with whips, the Foundation be suspended on wood; that Strength might grow weak; that the Healer might be wounded; that Life might die.[1]

Humility isn't timidity or weakness. If we've seen anything in the actions and words of Jesus, it's strength, but His strength was under control for a higher purpose. Having the same attitude as Jesus means that we, too, learn to be secure in the Father's love so that we can be radically committed to the Father's purposes. Paul explained to the Philippians that the reward for Jesus' faithfulness was praise and a position of honor at the right hand of the Father. In the same way, the reward for our faithfulness will be God's smile and blessings for all eternity. Not bad. Not bad at all.

Our attitude reflects what we value. If we value comfort and possessions, we'll be demanding and selfish. If we value popularity and prestige, we'll compete with people instead of loving them. But if we value God's love and God's purposes, we'll feel safe in His care and passionate about making a difference in others' lives.

• Activism

After perhaps the most beautiful and moving description of the character of Christ found in the New Testament letters, Paul explains what this attitude of humility looks like in action. He writes,

"Therefore, my beloved, as you have always obeyed, not as in my presence only, but now much more in my absence, work out your own salvation with fear and trembling" (Phil. 2:12 NKJV). Notice that Paul didn't say, "work *for* your salvation." He said, "work *out* your salvation." If God has really transformed out hearts and if we are truly gripped with the incredible reality of being forgiven and the experience of new life, then we'll want our actions to reflect the change in our hearts. We'll become activists, and our actions will reflect the life of Christ, because we'll increasingly "walk as He walked."

When we look at Jesus' activities in the Gospels, what do we see? On page after page, we see Him caring for "the least of these" and defending truth. As we increasingly are gripped with Jesus' attitude, our actions will become more like His. Instead of pursuing comfort and prestige, we'll intentionally pursue ways to help those in need. Instead of being annoyed by people, we'll increasingly look beyond the annoyance to see a person God treasures. And we'll extend a hand to touch the person or explain the truth of God's amazing grace.

If we can't love the people under our own roofs, then the compassion and power of God isn't real in our hearts.

In many ways, it's easier to be involved in hit-and-run activism by doing things for people across town or around the world, but showing God's love begins at home. If we can't love the people under our own roofs, then the compassion and power of God isn't real in our hearts. Quite often, we play the blame game with our spouse and kids more than with anybody else. I'm not saying they're perfect. They're not, but neither are we. But amazing things happen when I choose to lower my voice, speak words of affirmation, and see my family members as treasures instead of annoyances. Love, indeed, covers a multitude of sins—theirs *and* mine.

God also calls us to activism in the lives of people who cross our paths every day. Some of these people are friends who are easy to love, but some get in the way of our desire for speed and comfort. And some are just easy to ignore. How do you respond when . . .

○ a lady with a son with cerebral palsy is behind you in line at the grocery store?

○ you are approached by a pushy, stressed-out salesman?

○ you sit in front of a woman with a screaming child?

○ a secretary is quiet and withdrawn?

○ a client is sick and can't get back to you?

○ your clerk is so slow that every other check-out line looks like a racetrack?

○ the guy selling newspapers on the street asks you for the 597,394th time if you want to buy a paper?

○ you drive by homeless people under a bridge day after day?

○ the guy talking on his cell phone while he's driving cuts you off . . . again?

We've talked about the overflow of God's love, and it's a wonderful thing when God supernaturally gives us His love for someone who is hard to love. But in this passage, Paul tells us that loving others is obedience to God—whether we feel like it or not. Doing *what* God says to do *in the way* He wants us to do it is first and foremost a response to God's position of King and Master in our lives. We don't have much awe for government authorities in this country, but in Paul's day, the Roman emperor had supreme authority. People trembled in fear before him. Our King is incredibly kind, but He is still the Ruler of the universe. We obey Him because He deserves every ounce of our loyalty. He's earned it by His love poured out at the cross to forgive us, and He deserves it because He's the King.

• Authority

Here's the good news: God doesn't expect us to live lives of radical love and obedience on our own. He has given us the Holy Spirit to equip us and empower us. We trust in His authority, not our own. Paul wrote, "For it is God who works in you both to will and to do for His good pleasure" (v. 13 NKJV). This is a lesson all of us need to learn, and I'm no exception. Before the Spirit of God transformed my heart, all I cared about was me. I didn't give a rip about other people. I only cared what they could do for me. If they contributed to my success and happiness, that was cool. If not, I ignored them. But God changed my heart, and now I really love people. It's an amazing thing.

But my spiritual and emotional tank runs dry if I don't keep drinking of the Spirit's love and power. In fact, it runs dry pretty fast. As I draw close to Christ every day, I trust His Spirit to fill me again and again with compassion, direction, and strength. I need it . . . I desperately need it, because my old selfish nature is still alive and kicking (see Ephesians 4:20–24). Each day, I have a hundred opportunities to go in one direction or another—toward selfishness or toward love. I need the Holy Spirit's authority and compassion to fill me, direct me, and work through me. That's the only way I can walk as Jesus walked.

There are two views of the Christian life (actually, there are probably hundreds, but there are two main groups). One promises that if we are in tune with God, we'll breeze along in the Spirit. Everything will be easy, and God will make everything in our lives

smooth and successful. The other perspective promises that God will be with
us through good times and bad—and
we'll have plenty of both. Sometimes we'll
fly like eagles, and those are wonderful
moments in our lives. But we must also

*I warn people that
following Christ might
make their lives more
complicated—at least
for a while.*

trust God during the times when we're *running,* and even when
we're *walking* slowly along the path, God is leading us.

If we believe God will give us an effortless, always-successful life,
we'll be terribly disappointed. When things don't work out the way
we expect, we'll either blame ourselves for being so dumb or we'll
blame God for not coming through for us. But a life of faith is an
adventure filled with both joys and struggles, with both certainty
and mystery. In his classic book about the Christian life, *Knowing
God,* J. I. Packer observed that God has a higher purpose than helping us avoid pain. He wrote:

This is what all the work of grace aims at—an even deeper
knowledge of God, and an ever closer fellowship with Him.
Grace is God drawing us sinners closer and closer to Him. How
does God in grace prosecute this purpose? Not by shielding us
from assault by the world, the flesh, and the devil, nor by protecting us from burdensome and frustrating circumstances, nor
yet by shielding us from troubles created by our own tempera-
ment and psychology; but rather by exposing us to all these
things, so as to overwhelm us with a sense of our own inade-
quacy, and to drive us to cling to Him more closely. This is the
ultimate reason, from our standpoint, why God fills our lives
with troubles and perplexities of one sort or another—it is to
ensure that we shall learn to hold Him fast.[2]

One of my favorite recording artists is Frankie Beverly and his group, Maze. In an inspired moment, Frankie wrote this classic "hook" for his group's greatest hit: "Joy and pain are like sunshine and rain!" Both are part of an authentic walk of faith.

When Christian leaders promise that God will give people complete freedom from pain and make them healthy and wealthy, they're promising more than God intends to deliver—and that's pimpin'. Instead, I warn people that following Christ might make their lives more complicated—at least for a while. As they gradually replace lies with truth, manipulation with integrity, and selfishness with love, they'll face some difficult decisions. In fact, if things get tough for the right reasons, it means they're on the right path. It ain't easy, but it's the only life worth living.

ACTION, REFLECTION, ACTION

If we wait until we have perfectly pure motives and positive feelings before we take action, we won't do much. We have to get going, and we have to keep moving. Sooner or later, the feelings will follow. In his book, *Empowering the Poor*, Robert Linthicum calls this the "Action, Reflection, Action" model. The initial step is an act of faith. For instance, I know God has called me to care for "the least of these," so whether I feel loving or not, I take steps to reach out to care for a homeless person. As I get involved in his life, I reflect on this encounter, and God usually touches my heart with genuine love for him. That feeling of compassion propels me to take another step to help him, and quite possibly, to help many other people in need. Sometimes we obey

Sometimes we obey God's call because we feel like it, but sometimes we obey Him in spite of how we feel. Either way, God is honored.

God's call because we feel like it, but sometimes we obey Him in spite of how we feel. Either way, God is honored.

The same model applies to the larger scope in an organization. When we began our ministry at St. John's, we decided to take action to serve a meal to homeless and hungry people. After doing this for a while, we stepped back to reflect on what we were doing, and we learned a lot about God, about ourselves, and about the people we were trying to serve. We prayed and thanked God for the privilege of serving them, and we trusted Him for direction for the next step. The insights we gained during this time of reflection helped us become more effective in our next stage of action.

BENCHMARKS

I've heard it said that the measure of a man is what it takes to stop him. In the same way, the measure of our walks with God is how much we are active in loving "the least of these," who can't return the favor. In one of the most challenging statements in the Gospels, Jesus gave this instruction: "When you give a dinner or a supper, do not ask your friends, your brothers, your relatives, nor rich neighbors, lest they also invite you back, and you be repaid. But when you give a feast, invite the poor, the maimed, the lame, the blind. And you will be blessed, because they cannot repay you; for you shall be repaid at the resurrection of the just" (Luke 14:12–14 NKJV).

To how many people do you and I show love without an expectation of being repaid? The repayment we expect might not be by that person and it may not be "in kind." We might, though, expect people to notice how kind and generous we are, and their praise is plenty of repayment for us. But Jesus spoke to our hidden motives too. He said for us to give, love, and serve in secret:

"Take heed that you do not do your charitable deeds before men, to be seen by them. Otherwise you have no reward from your Father in heaven. Therefore, when you do a charitable deed, do not sound a trumpet before you as the hypocrites do in the synagogues and in the streets, that they may have glory from men. Assuredly, I say to you, they have their reward. But when you do a charitable deed, do not let your left hand know what your right hand is doing, that your charitable deed may be in secret; and your Father who sees in secret will Himself reward you openly" (Matt. 6:1–4 NKJV).

To how many people do you and I show love without an expectation of being repaid?

Caring for "the least of these" reveals our values and challenges our security. We have to be intentional, and we need to trust God to work in our hearts to take us beyond our comfort zones. Here are some suggestions:

o Ask God to open your eyes to see people the way He sees them—people in your family, at work, or in the neighborhood, and who cross your path each day.

o If people are annoying you, ask yourself, "What's going on in this person's life that might be causing him or her to need some attention?"

o Identify people who can't repay you for any acts of kindness you show.

o Take a step to physically touch three people today. Give a family member a hug; shake the hand of someone at work, at school, or in the neighborhood; and go out of your way to touch a person who is poor, sick, elderly, hungry, or wounded. Begin with shaking a hand. Perhaps later, you can touch an arm or give a hug. When we touch someone, a connection occurs that is categorically different—and more powerful—than spoken communication. Physical touch breaks down barriers and conveys warmth and acceptance more than any other way we connect with people. As we think about touching someone, some of us are afraid of getting germs. Yes, there may be germs, but you and I have them too. Jesus touched people. If we want to walk as He walked, we'll touch them. We simply can't have a real ministry to "the least of these" if we are afraid to touch people.

o As an extension of your love, remember the person's name. One of the things I've realized about myself and others is that we'll remember people's

> *We simply can't have a real ministry to "the least of these" if we are afraid to touch people.*

names if we care about them. One day I asked Juanita, "Do you have any trouble remembering a person's name if you love him?"

She thought for a minute and then shook her head. "No, I don't."

Not long ago, I realized that I'd met a young lady about six times, but each time, I couldn't remember her name. It was embarrassing, especially because she knew that I almost always remember people's names. After the sixth time, I stopped and asked myself why I was having such a problem, and the answer hit me: "It's because I don't care enough about her. I've been in a funk, and all I've been thinking about is myself. It's time to think about her as somebody God loves—and I love too." That did it. From that moment on, I was able to think about her life, her needs, her dreams, and I've never had a problem remembering her name again.

o Get up tomorrow and do it again. You may have to be intentional at first, but after a while, you'll develop a lifestyle of seeing people the way God sees them and reaching out to touch them.

RESISTANCE

We all have excuses for not doing what God wants us to do. Jesus heard them from men and women in His day. He hears them from us too: "I'm too busy." "This is harder than I thought." "I'll have to give up too much." "I've got my own plans." "What will my friends say?" These and a thousand other excuses get us off track. Most of our excuses center around our demand for safety. We are happy to follow Jesus as long as He doesn't ask us to do something that scares us. We're glad to follow Him as long as we can touch only clean, pleasant people who don't have too many germs. We're happy to follow Him as long as we can cling to the safety of our traditions, which don't require us to do anything out of the ordinary. And we're glad to follow Him as long as we are recognized as "wonderfully generous" or "especially kind" and "successful" in our efforts.

The vast majority of Christians have a "convoy mentality." Convoys only move as fast as the slowest ship. In the same way, we'll only give, love, and serve as much as the people around us—maybe a bit less, but certainly not more. Jerry Bridges, author of *The Pursuit of Holiness*, wrote:

Many Christians have what we might call a "cultural holiness." They adapt to the character and behavior pattern of Christians around them. As the Christian culture around them is more or less holy, so these Christians are more or less holy. But God has not called us to be like those around us. He has called us to be like himself. Holiness is nothing less than conformity to the character of God.[3]

Some forms of resistance are internal; some are external. Doubts, fears, and self-interest make us hesitate and second-guess our commitment to Christ and to ministry. And if we try to walk as Jesus walked, we might experience some of the same attacks that He suffered. Some accused Him of leading people astray, some said He was demon-possessed, and some of His best friends deserted Him in His time of need.

As we've seen, the chief threat to our commitment to love the way Jesus loved is our apparently insatiable thirst for the good life. Rich people don't come out looking too good in the New Testament. Oh, I know it's not that *money* is evil. It's *the love of money* that's the root of all evil. That's precisely my point: in our culture, we love money and what it can do for us. That affection for riches steals our affections, corrupts our values, and ruins our relationships.

Many of us have two problems. We pursue natural (often material) rewards instead of spiritual ones, and we demand to have our rewards right now instead of patiently waiting for some of them to come in God's timing. Do you remember the passage about doing good things in secret? The reason we want to tell the world about our kindness to others is that we want to be rewarded now for helping them. The point, Jesus was saying, is that rewards are promised either way. We can have the limited reward of public acclaim now, or we can have the untold riches of a reward from God later. It's our choice. The lust for more stuff is celebrated all around us. Billboards, radio and television commercials, and magazine ads tell us we deserve to have all we want, and we can't be happy unless we have it. It takes tremendous insight, courage, and faith to turn from those deceptive promises and turn to an invisible God and delayed rewards, but that's what God is calling us to do.

No, I'm not advocating that we become monks and nuns and live in poverty. The problem—and the solution—is primarily in our hearts. When our hearts are in tune with God, we'll care more about His passions. Things that used to seem so important will become insignificant. The amount of money a person has won't seem so important. The most important biblical insight about possessions is that everything we have is God's. He owns it all, and He has entrusted a little bit of His wealth to each of us. We are stewards, not owners, and that perspective changes how we use what God has entrusted to us.

> *The most important biblical insight about possessions is that everything we have is God's. He owns it all, and He has entrusted a little bit of His wealth to each of us. We are stewards, not owners, and that perspective changes how we use what God has entrusted to us.*

I've been pretty tough on the desire for riches as the primary goal of life, but some wealthy people in our church are wonderfully generous. They give a lot to our ministry, and they give with no strings attached. They don't want me to tell others what they've given. They are just happy to help expand the work of God at St. John's. These people love God with all their hearts—otherwise, they wouldn't stick around a place like this! My message to them is: "Thank you so much, and as God said to Adam and Eve, 'Be fruitful and multiply!'"

Over the last several years, I've talked to a lot of pastors and other church leaders from wealthy suburbs about God's call to love "the least of these." Let me distill these encounters into a composite conversation for you. As I explain our ministry focus and activities, Mr. Suburban Pastor seems to be tracking with me for a while, but then he says, "But, Rudy, you don't understand. People move to the suburbs precisely because they want to *get away* from drug addicts, homeless people, crime, and violence." He pauses for a moment. I can tell he's really thinking. Then he says, "You know, I don't think I even know any poor people."

I ask him, "Do you think that excuses you from Jesus' command to do things for people who can't repay and show love to 'the least of these'?"

He shrugs his shoulders in a dismissive way and says, "Well, if I'm not around them, how can I help them?"

I don't know whether to cry or cuss. I ask, "Are there any maids who clean houses in your neighborhood?"

He nods.

"Any lawn services?"

He nods again.

"Anybody selling papers on the streets?"

"Yes," he answers. The lights are starting to come on.

"Any old folks in nursing homes?"

"Yes," he tells me. "I do their funerals."

"So the only time you see them is when they're dead?"

I can detect a little defensiveness now. He reacts, "No, that's not the 'only time' I see them."

I press on. "How about alcoholics and drug addicts? You spend time with them, I'm sure."

He nods, "About twice a year, someone with a drinking problem comes to see me, and I refer him to a counselor in our city."

"Two people a year? How many people come to your church?"

He looks happy now that I'm talking his language. He tells me, "We have over a thousand people on most Sundays."

I look at him, wondering if he's pulling my leg. He isn't, so I continue. "Is there anyone in your neighborhood who is mentally challenged, with MS, cerebral palsy, or Down syndrome? Anybody with a family member in prison?"

He's getting a little hot now. "Rudy, you don't understand. I have a tremendous workload—preparing my sermons, leading committees, working with staff, the building program."

I'm not biting on the "too busy" excuse. "Brother," I tell him, "you have needy people all around you. You just don't see them. And maybe you don't want to see them because noticing them would call you to action, which would interfere with your neat, clean, ordered life."

I believe God has put it in the hearts of all true believers to love the unlovely.

That last comment might offend him, but I keep going. "And maybe, just maybe, God wants you and your people to take initiative to leave your safe, clean community to step into the world of the hungry and thirsty, naked, sick, and jailed. The limits of Jesus' command aren't what's comfortable and convenient. In fact, there aren't any limits to His command to touch the poor and needy."

As I've talked to suburban church leaders and members of their congregations about God's call for all of us to touch "the least of these" in our communities, many of them are resistant for a few minutes, but soon they get it. The lights come on, and their hearts resonate with this calling. I believe God has put it in the hearts of all true believers to love the unlovely. Instinctively, they know they need to be involved in this ministry; they just needed a reminder and a little push to take action.

ALONE, IF NECESSARY

I hope God will lead you to dozens of men and women who will be committed to walking as Jesus walked and touching the lives of "the least of these" in your community. Maybe He'll lead you to a few, maybe only one. But even if you have to take the first steps on your own, take them boldly with the assurance that your faith and action delight God's heart. As you step out to touch people, you can expect incredible things to happen, and as others see how God is using you, they'll want to join you. Together, then, God will use you to move mountains.

My willingness to accept people—to choose love over power or comfort—is tested all the time.

Henri Nouwen, the author of *The Wounded Healer*, was a thoughtful and compassionate man. He observed, "The long painful history of the church is the history of people ever and again tempted to choose power over love, control over the cross, being a leader over being led. Those who resisted this temptation to the end and thereby give us hope are the true saints." My willingness to accept people—to choose love over power or comfort—is tested all the time. Some people, I'll admit, are really hard to love. I can think of some people who almost drive me nuts, but every time I'm tempted to let my annoyance block God's love for them, I'm reminded that the night Jesus was born, the innkeeper rejected Him, and He had to be born in a stable. Years ago, Mother Teresa was asked how she could love so many people so much. She was obviously gripped with the truth of Jesus' affirmation, "Inasmuch as you did it to one of the least of these My brethren, you did it to Me" (Matt. 25:40 NKJV), so she replied, "Because they are Jesus." When I'm tempted to see someone as annoying or I think I'm too tired to reach out again, I look at that person and think, *That's Jesus.* That's my commitment, whether a thousand people join me or

I take these steps alone. Thankfully, God has put it in the hearts of His people to care for people in need, so I'm never alone.

A TOUCHING STORY: CHARLES WILLIAMS

 On Father's Day, 2001, I gave out our annual "Man of the Year" award. That morning, I told people I was giving the award to a man who had been touched by Jesus in a powerful way. That man, I told the congregation, was filled with Jesus' love, and he responded by loving Jesus and every person who came across his path. The recipient that year, I explained, was one of the most generous men I knew: Man of the Year, Charles Williams. And Charles just about had a heart attack!

You see, when Charles first started at St. John's, he was looking for fraud, looking hard for adulterers, thieves, hypocrites. He'd been clean and sober for sixty-five days, but he was still experiencing tremendous rage. His sponsor at Houston Aftercare had invited him to come to church at St. John's, but Charles angrily reacted, "Church can't help me!"

The sponsor patiently told him, "Maybe this one can."

The next Sunday morning, Charles and his sponsor walked into the back of St. John's sanctuary just as the choir was singing. Immediately Charles fell to the floor. For a long time, he lay there crying and hollering. He later explained, "I'd been running, but God caught me that morning."

He told me his experience with God that morning was powerful, but it didn't answer all of his questions. He was still skeptical—very skeptical—of church and anyone connected with it . . . like pastors. He explained, "For the next fifty-two weeks, I never missed a Sunday service. But I wasn't there to worship. I was there to find hypocrites, especially to see if the pastor was a hypocrite. I wanted to know if you were having an affair, if you were stealing money from the offering, or if you talked about caring for the poor but you had a big Cadillac around the corner. I was looking for fraud, and I was looking hard. But after fifty-two weeks, I didn't see any. Instead, God showed me the truth of His love through you and through the people at St. John's—and my life has never been the same."

Charles had been a stranger to this kind of love, and when he found it, it touched his heart. When he started coming here and feeling the love, he cried for weeks. He said he had never felt accepted in his life. He went though a treatment program, and the more sober he got, the more involved he became in the church's outreach. He told me, "Christ didn't come to be served, but to serve. And if I'm following Him, I'll serve too."

And that's why he was Man of the Year, 2001. Charles later told me that as he sat in church and listened that morning, he thought, *I don't know anybody like that, but I'd like to meet him!* But Charles is being modest, because he's a legend around here at St. John's. He was the addict who rode his bicycle about fifty miles from Galveston to Houston, seeking treatment for substance abuse. On the day Hurricane Rita threatened the destruction of Houston, he was one of several men who met me at the church to provide shelter for home-less people in our community. He has been involved in almost every area of our church's life: communions, baptisms, greet-ing people, and teaching Bible classes.

Charles's love for Jesus and his servant's heart haven't diminished in the thirteen years since he has been sober and Jesus touched his life. Today, he serves every way he can—not because he has to, but because he wants to.

PART 2
A Touch That Transforms a Church, a Community, and the World

CHAPTER 7
The Call on Crawford Street

"Lord, when did we see You hungry and feed You, or thirsty and give You drink? When did we see You a stranger and take You in, or naked and clothe You? Or when did we see You sick, or in prison, and come to You?' And the King will answer and say to them, 'Assuredly, I say to you, inasmuch as you did it to one of the least of these My brethren, you did it to Me.'" (MATTHEW 25:37–40 NKJV)

You draw a line down the center of a piece of paper and list the challenges and the needs on one side; you list the programs and the ministries that are designed to meet those needs on the other side. You assume that resources are no problem, and you cast visions accordingly. —KIRBYJON CALDWELL[1]

At St. John's, everything we do is designed to be inclusive. We are different. In fact, we are absolutely committed to breaking the mold, shaking up expectations, and changing norms. This ministry philosophy comes out of my own experiences before and after I trusted Christ to be my Savior. Before I became a Christian, I was as lost as anyone could be. My dad had taught me to be suspicious of anyone who was involved in organized religion, but still, I knew something was missing. I sure wasn't going to look to the church for answers, so I looked in other directions. At one point, I was a marginal Muslim; at another, I was a borderline Buddhist. In college, I had a spiritual advisor who was into Eastern mysticism. I was willing to try almost anything—anything but Jesus.

Before I became a Christian, I was suspicious about God and church folk. But Kirbyjon Caldwell modeled a life of honesty and integrity, and his example profoundly impacted me and shaped my approach to ministry. Through the dual lenses of "before and after," I have a greater grasp of God's purpose for St. John's and me as I respond to "His calling on Crawford Street."

LOOKING FOR FRAUD, FINDING GOD

I want to expand the story I told in Chapter 2 about God calling me to Himself and to ministry. After Juanita and I married, I was cool with her going to church, and after a while, I agreed to go with her. But I walked through the front door of Windsor Village United Methodist Church looking for fraud, not God. For months I listened for inconsistencies and watched for deception. To my great surprise, I didn't find anything like that. Then I had the opportunity to meet and talk with the pastor. Kirbyjon asked me what I did for a living. I told him about my real estate business, and I told him about our motel business. I was convinced that when I told him I ran a borderline bordello, he'd turn up his nose, walk away, and tell everybody to keep away from me—but he didn't. That impressed me. He was different from what I expected him to be, and that difference opened the door to me trusting him and, later, trusting God.

For many months I sat in the pew each week, watching and listening, but now my heart was open to Kirbyjon and his message about Jesus. I belonged to the church long before I believed in the Savior, but that was fine with the pastor. He never rushed me, and he never pushed me. He just loved me, even though he knew that my career was destroying lives every day. As we got to know each other, he even invited me to participate in meaningful ways at the church. I was starting to give money to the church's ministry, and he asked Juanita and me to give leadership to the stewardship program. Some people would say Kirbyjon shouldn't have put me in a leadership position at that point

For months I listened for inconsistencies and watched for deception. To my great surprise, I didn't find anything like that.

in my life, but his trust in me gave me opportunities to see up close the authenticity of the man and his ministry. He was (and is) the real deal, and the leaders of the church followed his example of integrity and accountability. He spoke the truth, and he did what he said he'd do. He lived what he preached. He never manipulated people; he treated them with respect and let them respond however they chose.

My suspicion gradually melted away, because in every encounter, my trust in Kirbyjon grew. Instead of showing up each Sunday looking for fraud, I came expecting to find God speaking to me through a man I trusted. In every service, I felt revived and encouraged. Then I went back into the darkness and destruction of my motel business, and during the week the flame of life would flicker and die. Week after week, month after month, the Sunday morning worship service was the point of light in my world of darkness.

After a long time of living in two worlds, Kirbyjon invited all the men to come to church one Wednesday night. He called it "Nothing But the Brothers." He divided up the group by zip codes, and we met together in smaller clusters of men. That's when I met Willie Lane and began attending his weekly Bible study on Thursday nights. Willie's Bible had more colors of highlighting than the rainbow. He had underlined some verses, highlighted others, and written notes all over that thing. It really impressed me that Willie wasn't shooting from the hip. He had really studied the Book. After a year of listening to Willie talk about the life of Jesus and the power of God's grace, I crossed over and trusted in Jesus.

EVERY PERSON, NO MATTER WHAT

The best word to describe my life before I met Jesus is *darkness*. The darkness I experienced not only clouded my own mind and heart; it also isolated me from people. It wasn't only that my own heart was in darkness—I was also a ringleader of darkness in the lives of other people. But now, God's light was illuminating my heart. I had compartmentalized my life so I could hide certain parts of me from people, but God's light shined on every part of my life and revealed some things that really needed to change. And now I wanted God to shine His light into the darkness around me.

> *I had compartmentalized my life so I could hide certain parts of me from people, but God's light shined on every part of my life and revealed some things that really needed to change.*

As I trusted God more, I was willing to let Him have His way with more and more of my life, and I began being more honest with others too. That was liberating. For the first time in my life, I felt free. For all of my adult life, I'd carried a gun, because I was certain that somebody somewhere would try to kill me. That wasn't paranoia. It was a reasonable, rational fear in our business. Two of my father's brothers had been murdered, and one of them had been in a business partnership with my dad. Fear may have been reasonable, but it consumed our lives. Dad tried to prepare me for attacks in two ways: by telling me to expect him to be murdered one day, and giving me a gun to protect myself. But God's love was shoving those fears aside.

I'm not sure I can explain all that happened to me in those first couple of years after I became a believer. God began to work in my life in a powerful way. I hadn't cared about people in pain, but now I started looking for them so I could do something to help them. It wasn't just a feeling; I got involved. I bought food for hungry people and paid some bills for those who couldn't afford things.

I no longer saw the young women who were selling their bodies for a few dollars simply as partners in our business. Now I realized they were dying inside. And I didn't see the men who used our motel as just customers; they were people who needed God's love. Men were destroying their families and themselves for a few minutes of pleasure, and many of them had no idea of the devastation they were causing. But now I knew. I'm not sure how I knew, but I knew—and it tore me up. I became convinced that each person— the addict and the suit, the call girl and the preacher, the homeless and the wealthy—is precious in the eyes of God. And if God can show His love *to me* and change *my* life, there's hope for *everybody*.

As the months went by, God worked His grace and His calling deep into my heart, and I felt the divine pull into ministry. I experienced tremendous tension between all that God was doing in my heart and my continued involvement in the motel business, and soon the strain reached a breaking point. Something had to give. That's when I surrendered my life completely to Jesus, and that's when my dad believed he had lost me. In that way, I traded one kind of pressure for another, but I knew I had to *resolve* the tension between God and me, even if it *created* tension between Dad and me.

I started watching two preachers on television, Robert Schuller and John Osteen. Those were the only two I watched, and I learned a lot from both of them. Almost every week, Dr. Schuller told people, "Find a need and fill it." I'd look at the television and shout, "Yeah! That's what the church ought to be doing!" John Osteen was Joel's father who founded and pastored Lakewood Church in Houston until his death a few years ago. When John Osteen preached, he looked right through the camera at me and said sincerely, "I just want you to know that I love you!" And I felt it. He even called his church the "Oasis of Love." I liked that. He told people, "I don't care what you've done or what you've been through, God loves you, and I love you." Kirbyjon's integrity and creative efforts to raise the spiritual and economic health of his members was my first and finest model in ministry. And from Schuller and Osteen, I learned to look for needs and fill them with genuine love. That was a powerful blend of heart and action, and that became my ministry model.

I have no room for any airs of superiority. With my background, my lifestyle, and my fears, my experience of God's grace is so rich and real I simply can't comprehend it all. And if God can love me like that, He must love everybody else in the same way. I had been the ringmaster of devastation, and now God was going to use me to repair some of the destruction I saw in people's lives. What an incredible honor! When I parked in front of St. John's the day Kirbyjon asked me to check it out, the only people I saw were the

> *I knew I had to resolve the tension between God and me, even if it created tension between Dad and me.*

homeless, helpless, and hopeless. They were exactly the kind of people God had put on my heart, people who were desperate enough to admit they needed help. Not all of them are "hungry, thirsty, naked, sick, and in prison"—"the least of these." Some are middle-class working people, and a few are wealthy, prominent citizens of our city. Our calling is to reach out to everybody who is open to God. When they cry out to God, He delights in using us to touch them.

That's my calling, my mission, my mandate, and my delight. On that first day and ever since, I knew the community around St. John's was my place to love people into God's kingdom. Most people—almost any sane person—would have been scared to death of this place: a rundown church in the middle of poor and homeless people. But God gave me an unmistakable sense that He was calling me to minister here. Before I ever walked in the door, Kelly and Maurice, two homeless men, met me on the sidewalk in front of the church. We talked, and I knew these two men were like angels sent from God to confirm His calling. That day, I began a relationship with these men who would become two of my best friends. Sometimes people just check out of their lives. They get up one day, take a last look around, and walk out. And then they never check back in . . . unable, for some reason, to escape the gravitational pull of life on the streets. That's the story behind Kelly and Maurice—my consultants and protectors in the early days on Crawford Street. They were always together; Maurice the leader, Kelly following.

The men had stopped by the church that late afternoon in 1992 to have a plate of cold spaghetti some kind soul was serving out of the back of a station wagon. They approached me as I literally stepped over the homeless sleeping in front of the church, and I sized them up quickly. The evident leader was tall—a couple inches over six feet, dark-brown skinned with short hair and a medium build. He moved like a statesman—confident with clear social skills. His buddy wasn't nearly as tall, but big bodied and big haired with a big belly—uncharacteristic of a hungry homeless person—and carried himself like a whole man. They packed light, wearing what they owned on their bodies—jeans, shirts, tennis shoes . . . the standard for an urban setting like Houston, where the homeless must constantly be on the move to avoid arrest for vagrancy.

Now, I grew up on the streets, so I know when I'm safe and I know when I'm in danger. These guys were safe. But there was much, much more to them. These men exuded dignity, and I found that intriguing. Dignity is the first thing you give up when you live on the street.

My first two years at St. John's, Kelly and Maurice were always there, always appearing together as if they were traveling companions. They were homeless, but they volunteered their time and expertise. Yes—expertise. Both men were academics, and Maurice had a degree in social work from a St. Louis university. They were very articulate and observant, and over time I realized they knew what they were talking about. They made appointments to see me and discuss their thoughts, sometimes in very formal dialogue—the way a consultant would approach a client. From personal, hands-on experience, they made suggestions to improve my programs, comparing our services to other downtown agencies, suggesting program enhancements and identifying potential problematic clients. They performed quality control for our hot-meal program, critiquing food quality, reporting instances of rudeness or disrespect toward others. They knew about shame, about living a life you should not be living. They knew about guilt, about *knowing* better, but not *doing* better. They knew how to reach people just like them.

And they looked out for me. The area homeless were surprised and suspicious when St. John's changed hands, and an unspoken tension radiated between the haves and the have-nots. Kelly and Maurice made sure I understood the cryptic code among those who struggled for survival in the streets. If a dispute developed among the clients, they were quick to remind the community that St. John's was a sanctuary from the streets and, therefore, respect was required. Because of these men and our track record of compassion, we've never had a break-in or burglary.

I loved these guys . . . two men who had been written off by the rest of the world, and we had wonderful conversations. And then, true to the transient nature of being homeless, they would disappear for periods of time. I wondered about them, worried about them. They were in their midthirties, resourceful, strong. People who live outdoors are extremely resilient. In the later years, Kelly disappeared completely, but popped up every now and then. He was a man whose self-respect was still intact in spite of his current circumstances, and a man with a deep love for his family. But Kelly was an addict, the guilt and toll of his drug-addled life etched on his face—a paradox of a man who loved his family but chose to live on the streets. By year five, I never saw Kelly again. And sure enough, barely forty years old, he ended up with diabetes and on dialysis, his body broken down, his life disintegrated. He left behind a wife and two children . . . and Maurice.

Maurice survived for six more years and, after a period of mourning, never mentioned Kelly again. We talked often. At first, he kept the details of his pre-Houston life veiled, as if he in no way wanted his family to find him. But the more we met, the more relaxed he became and started offering details. He told me his story, the classic "husband abandons family" tale. He mentioned his wife and daughter, his academic career, his life in St. Louis. And always, *always,* he was advocating for the street.

Many times Maurice would disappear for long periods and would resurface clean-cut and with a fresh perspective—an indication of either incarceration or a female friend providing housing. The last time he showed up, he was different. Sure, he was unsoiled and his hair was short, but he knew he was no better than anyone else. He was clear about his need to give back to our agency that had provided for him during times when he could not provide for himself. For six months, he volunteered four to five days a week in our kitchen, encouraging other homeless men in our environment to help out. Intimidated by fear, shame, or poor self-image, many men wait until the parking lot clears before they enter the church for a meal. Maurice understood these men who slipped off the edge, one hit too many, one motel room too many, one drink too many. He lured them off the sidewalk into St. John's and into mission work.

And then in the fall of 2004, on a slightly cool evening, we found Maurice dead at the back door of our church; the door that led to the kitchen and the only Houston family he knew. It took a while for the coroner to arrive and declare him dead. And an incredible thing happened as we waited. For two hours, while Maurice lay in state at St. John's back door, the entire homeless community passed by and paid their respects. Maurice was well respected, and functioned much like the mayor of the street. People came to him for advice, for help. He was their advocate, and he was not afraid to call out the officials doing a shabby job providing for the homeless. They wept at the loss of their leader. And I wept too. He was forty-five years old, dead of a heart attack, and his obituary confirmed everything he'd told me.

I will never forget that evening. And I will never forget Kelly and Maurice—two street angels who rallied around a young, in-experienced real estate broker with a heart for missions, took me under their wings, taught me, and encouraged me, to reach out and touch the untouchables.

THE THING ABOUT FEAR

People who knew me years ago told me later that I had looked like a man who kept secrets. They were right. In those days, I made a point of not letting people know what was going on with me. In my motel business, the fewer people who knew about me, the safer I'd be, so I made sure no one knew my business. I was afraid that if people knew too much about me, they'd ridicule me or try to hurt me. Fear is sometimes understandable, but it prevents us from giving and receiving love. Our ministry at St. John's is all about including every person and sharing God's great love, so part of our mandate is to identify fears and replace them with trust. That's the only way I know to clear out the channels of the heart clogged by fear so that God's love can flow.

Our ministry at St. John's is all about including every person and sharing God's great love, so part of our mandate is to identify fears and replace them with trust.

People who live in fear long for safety and control. Some of us try to control our pain by medicating it with drugs or alcohol, and some of us try to control it by our drive to succeed so no one can ever ridicule or reject us. Some of us are convinced we're scum, and we're terrified anybody will find out. To defend ourselves, we live behind barriers of deceit, telling lies and hiding our secrets. If anybody really knew us, we're sure, they'd make fun of us, or worse, abandon us. Fear causes some of us to run away, some to hide, some to give in quickly to avoid conflict, and some to fight back.

Anger looks like the dominant emotion in many people's lives, but I think anger is a surface emotion. The deeper feeling, the root of that anger, is the fear of being alone, being rejected, and being a failure. We lash out at anyone or anything that threatens us, and we use blame, withdrawal, and all kinds of other punishments to get back at those who have threatened us. If we live in fear, we keep trying to protect ourselves, but we keep getting hurt again and again. We try even harder to control people so they can't hurt us again, but they don't like being controlled, so they get angry with us and threaten us again—and the cycle continues.

Being successful, having great stuff, and winning popularity promise to soothe our fears—and they do, for a moment. But fear soon raises its demanding, consuming head and tells us we aren't good enough, smart enough, or pretty or handsome enough. We can't get enough power or control people enough to make the fear go away. We can't numb enough of the pain or please people enough. The fear is still there consuming our lives. The solution to our destructive, nagging fear isn't playing the game better. It's to look at the brutal truth of our deepest fears—not deny them or disguise them—and realize we are desperate for love to conquer our fears.

That's what I found in Jesus, and that's what my life and ministry are all about.

Love always involves risk. Love speaks the cold, hard truth of our condition: we are deeply loved but tragically fallen. Jesus didn't gloss over the fact of our sinfulness and that we'd perish if we didn't trust in Him, but He didn't stand apart from us and condemn us. He stepped into our world, identified Himself as one of us, and paid the terrible ransom to set us free. He spoke to the deepest parts of our hearts and said, "Peace I leave with you, My peace I give to you; not as the world gives do I give to you. Let not your heart

Love always involves risk.

be troubled, neither let it be afraid" (John 14:27 NKJV). The peace the world offers is conditional, based on us having enough possessions, prestige, or popularity to make the fear go away. But it's never enough. Jesus' peace is free and full of truth. It addresses our deepest fears, not with superficial substitutes, but with His deep grace, love, forgiveness, and strength.

I believe every person who comes to my office or to our church is tainted to some degree by fear. That's not a condemnation, just an accurate evaluation of the human condition. Fear blocks love. My fear of pastors and church people led me to put up a barrier to keep them and God out, but God used a few faithful, trustworthy people to change my heart so I could be open to His love.

As I meet with men and women every day, I find their hearts are either like sponges or bricks. Some, like Charles Williams, are instantly touched when they experience God's love. They soak it up like a sponge! Charles was so overwhelmed with the new feeling of being loved that he cried for weeks. His tears were, I believe, joy and relief—the joy of feeling the love and relief that he didn't have to keep hiding his pain anymore.

But many others have hearts like bricks. I was like that. These people need the steady touch of love, grace, and truth day after day, week after week, until their hearts are gradually broken and they can absorb the living water of God's love. Because I was like this, it doesn't surprise me a bit when people don't get it the first time they walk through our doors. Every encounter with God's people and God's love, though, chips another grain or two off the brick. Sooner or later, the broken pieces will be as absorbent as a sponge.

Whether people are sponges or bricks, we are committed to loving them. Some immediately soak it in, and some are more hesitant, but the fact that they come tells me that they long to love and be loved. That's why we tell each person each week, "I love you, and there's nothing you can do about it!"

DIFFERENT, REALLY DIFFERENT

When Juanita and I came to St. John's, Kirbyjon gave us complete freedom to shape our ministry the way we felt God was leading us. As soon as we began, we determined to be a little different—actually, *really* different. Even though Kirbyjon had modeled a life and a ministry of integrity, I still inherently didn't trust the institutional church. I trusted him completely, and I greatly admired his ministry at Windsor Village, but I was still haunted by my dad's suspicion of the institutional church. I never wanted anybody to experience St. John's and be turned off because it looked, tasted, and felt too stiff and dry. I told Kirbyjon I wanted St. John's to be completely casual so every person—rich and poor, enfranchised and disenfranchised, sober and high, black and white, straight, gay, and lesbian—would feel comfortable looking to God together. He was cool with that.

I wanted St. John's to be completely casual so every person—rich and poor, enfranchised and disenfranchised, sober and high, black and white, straight, gay, and lesbian—would feel comfortable looking to God together.

The previous pastor at St. John's, Jerry Stith, had already opened the door to the homeless people in the community, so when Kelly and Maurice began telling people to come to church, the barriers had already been broken down, and they came. We also hired a couple of homeless people to help us serve a meal each week, and that helped us build trust with people living under the bridge. Our ministry of serving meals was called "Bread of Life," but we soon noticed that food wasn't the only thing these people needed. Many of the homeless people we served needed a place to take a shower, so we gave them a place where they could clean up. And we soon realized many of those we served needed medical care, so we opened a clinic staffed with volunteer nurses and doctors. As we provided this care we realized that some who came to us were either infected with HIV-AIDS or affected by a family member who was sick with this dread disease. The City of Houston asked if they could put a clinic in our church to test people for the virus, and I knew just the right man to run the clinic. Stan Phils had come to our church as a homeless, helpless cocaine addict, but God had touched his life in a powerful way. Stan has a tender heart for hurting people, and he has a wonderful gift for administration. He was the perfect choice to run the clinic, and he proved the point by testing far more people than the city projected for our clinic. When we began at St. John's, we knew God wanted us to start the Bread of Life to feed people, but we had no idea that this ministry would evolve into so many services for those God wanted us to touch. (To find out how your church can reach out to homeless people in your community, read the appendix, "How to Begin a Ministry to Homeless People.")

From the beginning, our worship service was really relaxed, almost like a nightclub on Sunday. We wanted people to feel at home and have some fun at church. We wanted to minimize formality and eliminate anything that felt rigid and awkward. If people weren't familiar with church rituals, we sure didn't want them to feel embarrassed, so we had almost no rituals at all. By the time the *Chronicle* article hit the streets, people streamed through the doors to be a part of what God was doing.

The "pioneers" who came over from Windsor Village really helped us get going strong. In those early days, we relied heavily on these wonderful volunteers. I don't know what we would have done without people like Jonathan and Connie Gregory, Pat and Helen Patterson, and Jocelyn Noland. In the first weeks, Jonathan and Connie put the bill for the weekly meal for the hungry on their credit card. Pioneers love to start things, but they don't like bureaucracy. After a few months of growth at St. John's, we had so many people that we had to get organized. At that point, some of the pioneers lost interest and left to start another church, and the "settlers" helped us organize our ministry so it could run more smoothly and be more effective.

We are intentionally counterculture—counter-*church*-culture, that is. We aren't trying to be different just to be different. I wanted to touch the people nobody else was touching, so I was fiercely committed to making them feel comfortable. Here are a few things we do at St. John's to fulfill God's mandate to be inclusive:

- ## We advocate diversity on the pew.

We promote diversity by economic status, marital status, race and ethnicity, age, sexual orientation, and every other conceivable group of people. We actively invite them all. Some people say that you can't determine who comes to church, but I believe you can. We pay homeless men and women three dollars to come to church each week. To have a real feel for the kingdom of God, I want somebody who stinks to sit next to somebody who doesn't. It's not that big a deal, really. If you went to church in a Third World country, that's what you'd find. I'm just bringing the world to St. John's, but I don't have to go very far because they live under the bridge next to us.

To have a real feel for the kingdom of God, I want somebody who stinks to sit next to somebody who doesn't.

- *We defend each person's right to come to church.*

From time to time, an enfranchised person comes to me to complain about the addicts or homeless people. In those conversations, I am the champion of the underdog. I try not to use the same language Jesus used when He defended the common people against the self-righteous condemnation of the "group that's always right," but I let them know that the people they are complaining about are my honored guests—no question about it. It's interesting that the addicts and homeless people never complain about the self-righteous attitudes of some enfranchised people. I haven't figured out the reason for that yet, but it's true.

Others who complain are people who have struggled for years with a habit or an addiction and have gotten clean and sober. After a few months, they can't remember what it was like to be a lying, stealing, manipulative, irresponsible addict, and they are quick to condemn people who are still struggling. Sometimes one of them will come to me and say, "Pastor Rudy, what are you going to do about those homosexuals (or addicts or cross-dressers or mentally ill people)?"

I want to slap them, but I tell them, "Brother, you need to show them the same unconditional love and grace we showed you when you were smoking crack and sitting in the pew week after week—for years! You didn't have anywhere to go, and we took you in. That gay man doesn't have a church to go to because he feels condemned everywhere he goes, and we're going to show him some love."

- *We serve food in the sanctuary.*

We wanted to demystify church, and the best way to do that was to turn the sanctuary into a cafeteria and the pews into dining tables. I've found that if people are fed in a room, they feel more relaxed when they worship God in that room.

- *Food is the gathering imperative.*

If we want people to feel at home and be relaxed, we need to serve them something to eat. Sometimes it's a full-spread banquet, and sometimes we just serve snacks. The stomach is the door to people's hearts.

- *We want to attract creative, competent people to partici-pate in ministry.*

One of the greatest joys of leading people is seeing the thrill on their faces when they sense God is using them to touch lives. At St. John's, God has brought us some wonderful men and women to lead in every aspect of our ministry. My job (and my joy) is to notice their gifts, find places for them to serve, provide resources, give them enough authority so they own their roles, and encourage their socks off. We talk often about God using us to change lives. That's the motivation for excellence, and it shows in their hard work, their joy in serving, and their heartfelt prayers for God to use their efforts.

- *We touch people.*

Figuratively and literally, we touch people in all kinds of ways. At St. John's, it starts in the parking lot when our "ambassadors" reach out to shake people's hands. In the worship service, we hug people. To be honest, it startles some people when an addict or a homeless person hugs them the first Sunday they come to church here. It's a part of our culture of caring, and it communicates the warmth in God's kingdom. Some people, it's true, don't feel comfortable, and they withdraw from being hugged. But, if they'll stick around, they might find that their walls come down and the hugs touch them more deeply than they ever imagined.

When we serve a meal on Sundays, we used to do all the cooking in the kitchen near the balcony during the eleven o'clock service. One day I was preaching, and something in the kitchen caught on fire. Smoke filled the kitchen, then spilled out into the balcony. I looked up from the pulpit and calmly said, "Fire?" In an instant, the crowd was ready to hit the doors as if they were Olympic high jumpers!

Four times in one year, a lady collapsed and her muscles became rigid during the service, just about the time I was beginning the sermon. Each time, I stopped the service and got some brothers to carry her out to a room near the sanctuary, and we called the paramedics to give her aid. While the brothers and the lady waited for EMS to arrive, she told the men where she felt she needed to be rubbed, and these good men gave her a massage to relieve her pain. By the fourth event, I had a hunch there was more to it than a medical problem. That time, the brothers carried her out, but I asked some sisters to attend to her. She didn't want those women rubbing on her. Suddenly, she was miraculously healed, and she walked away!

One Sunday, my friend Christian Washington was preaching about repentance. We gave people a sheet of paper for them to write down their sins and bad habits, and then we invited them to come down and put them on the altar to claim God's forgiveness. People started writing right away. Christian also told people that if they wanted to stop smoking, *Somebody had thrown a butcher knife up on the stage!* they could toss their packs of cigarettes or weed on the altar. He invited them to bring to the altar anything that was blocking their relationship with God. After a few minutes, the front of the church looked like a sea of white paper and packs of cigarettes. Suddenly, we heard a loud thud. Somebody had thrown a butcher knife up on the stage!

A man came up to us after the service and told us that he had planned to hurt somebody with that knife, but God had touched his heart that morning, and he changed his mind. It was true repentance.

Jesus didn't demand that people clean up their acts before He met with them to show them His love. He hung out with all kinds of people, especially "the least of these," and He invited all of them to trust Him. As He loved people that way, some really strange things happened to Him. As we've tried to follow Him, some strange things have happened to us too. That's part of the deal, and I love it.

A TOUCHING STORY: STAN PHILS

Early on a cold September morning, Stan was sleeping on a sidewalk in front of the Star of Hope Mission in Houston. A guy sleeping next to him woke up and asked Stan, "What do you think the Rockets are gonna do today?"

This seemingly insignificant comment shook Stan. He remembered, "I was twenty-seven years old, sleeping on the street, my wife had left me because I'd ruined my life with drugs and alcohol . . . and all the guy next to me—in the same condition I was in—could think of was a basketball team. I started crying at the hopelessness of my life. I lost it that day."

Another homeless man saw Stan was crying. He told him, "Man, it'll get better. Go with me to a church where we can get a meal. We'll sit through a Cocaine Anonymous meeting; then they'll feed us." The two men walked to St. John's.

Stan told a friend, "My whole life changed that day. When

I came to the door of the CA meeting, a man met me at the door. He was a little guy, but he gave me a big hug. I was shocked because I hadn't had a bath in a week, and I stank. I couldn't imagine anybody *getting near me*, much less *hugging* me in a warm, strong embrace. That man was Rudy Rasmus."

As he sat in the CA meeting that day, Stan heard things about addiction that he'd never heard before. Suddenly, things started making sense. He told the friend, "After the meeting, I talked to two men who led the meeting, and they helped me get into treatment only a few days later. As soon as I got out of treatment, I got back to St. John's as quickly as possible. I talked to Rudy, and he said something that blew me away. He told me that he saw 'tremendous potential' in me. I could hardly believe it. I had dropped out of school in the eighth grade, and I couldn't read very well. I'd lived my life in shame, so I hadn't seen *any* potential in myself."

As Stan got more involved in St. John's recovery ministry, an amazing thing happened: he realized that God had given him a gift to help hurting people. I met with Stan regularly, and we developed a really close relationship—we weren't *like* brothers; we *were* brothers. Soon he was leading a CA meeting, the very meeting he came to that first day when he came in from the slab. He often tells people, "Once you realize your gifts, you'll find your purpose. And when you know your purpose, you can fulfill your destiny. My gift is to help people in pain, and my purpose is to serve people in our community so they can find hope and healing. My destiny is to make a difference in the lives of people. It all started with a hug at the door of St. John's."

Someone at the church tutored Stan, and he passed his

high school equivalency exam the first time he took it. His thirst for knowledge led him to enroll in the University of Houston in a program on drug addiction counseling.

While he was attending college, I called him with a unique opportunity that fit him perfectly. Because so many street people came to St. John's, the City Health Department wanted to start a pilot program at the church to test homeless people for HIV and syphilis. Stan was God's man to run that program. The Health Department set quotas for testing, and Stan exceeded those goals by double or triple. People could leave after the church service on Sunday morning and walk into our clinic at the church for testing. It was a unique situation.

In his testing, Stan found a number of people who needed medical care or drug treatment, but he faced a dilemma. Reputable facilities had long waiting lists, and the ones that had spots available often weren't competent. Either way, the people who needed help weren't getting it. Stan told me, "It tore me up that I couldn't help them." God put it on Stan's heart to build a transitional housing unit for these people who needed care. For this to happen, Stan would have to take a leap of faith. He left the staff of St. John's and started his own ministry called "A Caring Safe Place."

In the last few years, God has been doing amazing things in and through Stan's life. His ministry is flourishing, and he just opened a multimillion-dollar facility for men infected with HIV. During this time, he graduated from the University of Houston in addiction studies. In addition, he received his associate's degree from the College of Biblical Studies, which is affiliated with Dallas Theological Seminary, and recently, he earned a bachelor's degree in leadership with a 3.5 grade point average.

"Tremendous potential." Stan couldn't see it in himself that day he—as a homeless, hopeless man—came in off the slab into a CA meeting at St. John's. But his God-given ability only needed to be noticed and nourished with love and truth for it to become a reality. Stan tells people, "If anybody who comes to St. John's wants to know where their money is going, tell them to look at me. If they're wondering if the church is helping anyone, they can talk to me. Like countless others, I'm a product of the mission statement, the love, and the truth that St. John's is all about."

CHAPTER 8
Keeping It Real

"Nor do [people] put new wine into old wineskins, or else the wineskins break, the wine is spilled, and the wineskins ruined. But they put new wine into new wineskins, and both are preserved." (MATTHEW 9:17 NKJV)

As long as I am constantly concerned about what I "ought" to say, think, do or feel, I am still the victim of my surroundings and not liberated. . . . But when I can accept my identity from God and allow Him to be the center of my life, I am liberated from compulsion and can move without restraints. —HENRI NOUWEN

One of the most terrifying moments in my ministry at St. John's happened about four months after we began. Those months were electric. We were trying things I'd never even seen before, reaching out to homeless people, addicts, cross-dressers, and anybody else who would walk through our doors. The wonderful people who came from Windsor Village to help us were just as excited as Juanita and I, and they gave every ounce of their hearts and energy to touch people's lives. People came . . . and more people came. Suddenly, there were so many people that we couldn't just do "the God thing" on the fly anymore. We had to organize!

At that moment, we were threatened with becoming an institution instead of a movement.

TRANSITIONS

The history of the Christian faith shows us many examples of cutting-edge movements God used to change lives. Each of them began with a person or a small group of people who looked at the current condition of the church and concluded, "We ain't gonna put up with this mess anymore! Let's trust God to do something about it." Sometimes their holy disgust was focused on the deadness of the institutional church, and sometimes their hearts broke when they saw all the lost people who weren't being reached for Christ. They said, "Enough is enough!" And they took action. People like Augustine, Francis of Assisi, Ignatius, Luther, Calvin, Count Zinzendorf, John Wesley, John Mott, Billy Graham, and others shaped Christian history with their zeal to make a difference.

All movements start fresh and real. The first people to join are pioneers who are thrilled with the challenge of starting something new. They realize that, in some way, the old organizational wineskins have broken, and they are determined to put the new wine of their enthusiasm and vision into new wineskins, which are innovative practices that make a difference.

Sooner or later, however, the success of these movements challenges their foundational assumptions. The initial zeal has to be harnessed and channeled so it can be effective for even more people, but the organization created to harness and channel that zeal can strangle it. At that pivotal point in their history, each movement is faced with a monumental threat and an opportunity: to move through a transition from infancy to maturity (or at least adolescence) by creating new norms. For the movement to survive and thrive, vision and zeal cannot be sacrificed. They must be protected, and even enhanced, by the newly created systems and practices. Some of the movements in church history became cutting-edge organizations, but others turned into rigid, dead bureaucracies.

That was our challenge at St. John's. We had to find a way to keep it real as we grew. We've tried hard—and to be honest, we've struggled—to keep our ministry as fresh as the day we opened the doors. In this chapter, I want to share some of the things we've done to stay fresh and real.

MY FILTER

The assignment God has given me is to find and touch people who are ready to respond to Him. He has given me a gift of discernment to recognize what's in people's hearts, but He's also given me another tool: my braided beard. My beard is a filter to see how open people are to me and my message, and it saves me from wasting a lot of time with negative, judgmental people. When people come into my office or if I'm waiting on a flight at the airport, the reaction of people to my beard indicates their openness. When people look at me, I can read their faces like a billboard. The look on some of

> *He has given me a gift of discernment to recognize what's in people's hearts, but He's also given me another tool: my braided beard. My beard is a filter to see how open people are to me and my message, and it saves me from wasting a lot of time with negative, judgmental people.*

their faces says, "Hey man, that's cool. I want to get to know you and see what you're all about." But the look on other faces screams, "Danger! Crazy man in the vicinity! Get away as fast as possible." And they do. In my office, they check their watches or cell phones and tell me they have to rush off to an important appointment, and at the airport, they hide behind their magazines and sit as far away from me as they can. The Scriptures say that man looks on the outward appearance, but God looks at the heart. In my case, people look at my outward appearance, and their reaction shows me their hearts.

NEW NORMS

I can't tell you how many times at St. John's we've stepped back and asked, "Are we losing it? Are we becoming a rigid, lifeless institution? How can we keep it fresh and real?" Our goal is to be radically inclusive so that every person who even thinks about coming will feel welcome. To accomplish this . . .

• *We treat all people with the same level of respect.*

We have a lot of "the least of these" at St. John's, but we have plenty of middle-class and upper-class members too. Human nature tells me to give special attention to someone who drops a big check into the offering plate, or to Beyoncé, or to a political leader. But we're committed to treat the addict who comes in from under the bridge with the same attention, love, and honor as we give to big givers and stars. We don't designate certain pews for people who give a lot of money, and we don't point out how much they give. In the same way, we don't disparage the gifts we get from a homeless person. We've had food stamps put in the offering plate. That's the "widow's mite," and it warms my heart.

• *We demand little and expect much.*

People can come as long as they want to come, without giving a dime or helping in any of our ministries. If they just want to come and soak up some love, that's fine with me. In fact, that's great! But I expect God to transform their lives. His Spirit is at work, and He's doing all kinds of incredible things to change attitudes and actions. My expectations, though, are focused on God, not on people. He'll work in and through people if we keep loving them unconditionally and consistently. The transaction in their hearts may take a while—negotiations often do. But that's up to God and that person, not me.

When God works in a person's heart, real change happens. Our job is to point people to Jesus and invite them to open their hearts to Him. We expect people who respond to Him to repent, to genuinely turn from sinful behavior to doing what's right. I've had a young man come forward in a spirit of repentance and hand me his pistol. He had planned to shoot somebody, but God changed his heart. To him, repentance meant giving up the instrument of evil he had in his pocket. We never tell people what repentance *should* mean or what they *ought* to do. I believe sane people know the difference between right and wrong, sin and righteousness, acceptable and unacceptable behavior.

> *We never tell people what repentance should mean or what they ought to do. I believe sane people know the difference between right and wrong, sin and righteousness, acceptable and unacceptable behavior.*

If I try to define it for people by giving examples, I might limit God's work in their lives. I simply tell them that sin is anything that separates them from God. I don't make assumptions that anyone has given up everything that is hindering their relationship with God. I leave it to the Spirit and that person's conscience to work out the details, and that has worked pretty well.

I often remind the congregation that St. John's is a family that loves Jesus. If they want to join our family, we welcome them. They can belong from the first day they come, but we don't require them to love Jesus like we do. They can hang around and watch and be loved as long as they want. When they sense God is touching them, they can reach out and grab His hand in faith. But we don't rush them; they can *belong* as long as they want until they *believe.* That's my story, and that can be their story too. The disciples were with Jesus for a good while before any of them made a christological statement. They belonged to His group for a long time before they believed in Him. Yes, I know that "the church" technically contains only those who have placed their faith in Christ. But in my own mind, at least, I've expanded the definition at St. John's to be a family that welcomes anyone who will come: preachers and prodigals, the obedient and the searching.

• *We require respect for people and property.*

We don't have any rules about coming to church, giving money, or anything like that, but we have some hard and fast rules about every person being treated with dignity. Our struggle against injustice isn't just an abstract political position; we fight against any and every form of injustice in our church family. We require that each person who comes to St. John's respects every other person and their property. That means we don't allow panhandling at the church, and it means homeless people aren't allowed to defecate on the sidewalk around the building. We've asked the people who live on the streets in our community to help protect the church, and we've never had a break-in or any damage from vandalism. As we respect each person, each learns to respect him- or herself and others. Our rules may be few, but they're important.

- *We help people empathize with those who are struggling.*

Sometimes people look at our ministry and say things like, "Why do you spend so much time with addicts, bums, and prostitutes? They need to clean up their acts before they come to church." People who say things like that have never spent the night under a bridge without a penny in their pockets. They've never awakened and wondered where they've been the last several days. And they've never hated themselves for giving their bodies to a fat, sweaty guy who used them like a toy. These people are dying by inches every day, and we extend life support. Most of the enfranchised can't understand because they haven't experienced needs like these, so it's our job to educate their minds as God transforms their hearts. We want to help them learn to care, but caring for a few minutes isn't enough. People who are outcasts have spent years living self-destructive, mind-numbing lives. Part of empathy, then, includes understanding that it often takes a long time for love to make a dent in a hopeless, hardened heart. I've seen people who hung around our church for ten years with no visible change in their lives, but suddenly, something clicked, and they got it. And we celebrated!

> *I've seen people who hung around our church for ten years with no visible change in their lives, but suddenly, something clicked, and they got it. And we celebrated!*

- *We don't care what people look like.*

Years ago I was the guest speaker at a church, and after the message, a young man came forward to give his life to Christ. He had been smoking and dealing crack, so this was a big step for him. He was dressed in a starched, ironed shirt and some nice jeans. The pastor stood next to me that morning. He shook the man's hand and told him, "I'm giving you the hand of fellowship this morning, but next week, I want you to come back wearing some nice clothes." I was horrified. That experience galvanized my conviction that we'd always be relaxed in what we wear, and we'd never, ever make fun of anything anyone wears. Every Sunday, I wear jeans and a baseball cap, so we've eliminated any perceived dress code. The fact that I wear jeans also lowers a barrier for people who want to come to church, especially for men to feel comfortable coming to church—and that's huge.

- *We're loud, and we love to laugh.*

People enjoy concerts because they're bigger than life, and they enjoy comedy clubs because they love to laugh. The church is neither a rock concert nor a comedy routine, but we want to draw something from both environments. I want to give people a place to holler. It liberates them and makes them feel alive. Years ago, Joni Mitchell sang a song that said, "Laughing and crying is the same release." We laugh a lot because we have a lot of pain and we need some relief. We cry a lot, but that gets old. Laughing and crying in church bring healing and give us shared, heartfelt experiences. These times draw us closer together. A suburbanite who came to our church told me that he'd never laughed so hard at church in his life. He said, "The theology was right-on, the personal applications were specific, and the laughter made it all go down really well."

- *We baptize people in street clothes.*

This practice may not sound important to people from some

denominations, but it's important to many of us. In some traditions, people change from their church clothes to robes, and if the women don't want to mess up their hair, they wear swim caps. I've seen some women ready to be baptized who looked as though they were dressed for scuba diving! Nothing was going to get wet but their faces. But at St. John's, we welcome anyone who wants to declare to the world that Jesus is Lord. They don't have to wear a robe or a wet suit or anything else. We take them just as they are. And we also don't make a big deal of the amount of water used in the baptism. Some want to be sprinkled, and some want to be dunked. The issue is their faith in Jesus Christ. If they aren't serious about doing business with Him, dunking them in the Gulf of Mexico won't do any good!

• We stay connected.

A lot of people are easier to spend time with than addicts, the mentally ill, gang members, and others who are on the fringe of society. I need to select, equip, and shepherd ministry leaders, but not at the expense of spending quality time with people on the edge. For me, the demands of a growing church scream for me to take more and more time to organize, plan, and orchestrate the ministry. I have to do those things, but to avoid getting out of balance, I analyze my schedule every week to be sure I stay in touch with our primary audience. Success can lead to isolation, and I can't let that happen.

> *I need to select, equip, and shepherd ministry leaders, but not at the expense of spending quality time with people on the edge.*

• We are rigorously nonpolitical.

Jesus had every opportunity to align himself with the political parties of His world, but He refused to get involved. In His day, the Sadducees were a religious group that defined themselves by what they *didn't* believe: They didn't believe in the Spirit, angels, or the resurrection of the dead at the end of time. The Sadducees advocated a policy of accommodation with the Roman authorities to keep conflict at a minimum. The other major party, the Pharisees, were religious traditionalists and strict constructionists of the Jewish culture, who wrote hundreds of additional rules to control the behavior of their followers. Two parties—one trusted big government, and the other tried to control choices. It sounds familiar, doesn't it? They each tried to bait Jesus to take sides and make statements about taxes, Roman authority, and religious traditions, but He wouldn't take the bait. He told them, "Render . . . to Caesar the things that are Caesar's," and "My kingdom is not of this world" (Matt. 22:21; John 18:36 NKJV). He condemned each side equally for not pursuing God with a pure heart and for refusing to care for people in need. Jesus' eyes were fixed on God's purposes, and neither party could get Him off track.

That's my policy too. We don't endorse political candidates, and we don't support parties. We do, however, take positions on a few issues that affect our people. For example, the city of Houston passed two ordinances that I opposed because they hurt homeless people. One stated that it is unlawful for any person to put anything on the sidewalk during certain times of the day. The other forbids people with "offensive body odors" from going to the public libraries. I fought both of these tooth and nail because they hurt people God cares about.

For any ordinance, we need to ask, "What are the implications of the law for 'the least of these'?"

For any ordinance, we need to ask, "What are the implications of the law for 'the least of these'?" The sidewalk ordinance is arbitrary because a businessman who puts his briefcase down is just as guilty as a homeless woman who drops her bedroll. But who do you think they'll cite? For the library "smell test," city officials obviously made an assumption that if a person stinks, he's homeless. That's not necessarily true, but even if the person is homeless, he may need to go to the library to do some research to find a job, or he may be cold and need to come in to get warm. Either way, that person deserves some respect and understanding. My question was, "How do you quantify what is offensive?" The city officials had no definitive answer. It seems that any librarian who has a sensitive nose can kick out anybody who doesn't smell like springtime. These librarians can make their own arbitrary assessment about each person who walks in the door, and they then refuse the right to use a public building to someone who needs it. That's not right.

We don't take political stances on presidential candidates or the controversial issues of the day, but we take firm stands on behalf of people in peril. They say, "All politics is local." That's certainly true for us. Our right and our duty are to fight against injustice that affects the men and women, boys and girls we care about. If I take a strong position about the death penalty, abortion, or homosexual marriage, I risk alienating a

> *My calling is to love people into God's kingdom. Making them angry over a political issue doesn't accomplish my calling.*

segment of my audience who needs to hear the gospel and come to Jesus. I know some church leaders disagree with my position on this, but I'm convinced it's the path Jesus modeled for us. My calling is to love people into God's kingdom. Making them angry over a political issue doesn't accomplish my calling.

A lady from Washington came to our church one Sunday. She was an advocate of gay rights, and she wanted me to support her cause. After the service, she came up to me and said, "Pastor, I saw some couples in the church this morning who are obviously gay, and they look like they feel right at home here. I like what you're doing to support gay rights."

I responded, "Wait just a minute. Did you also see plenty of couples this morning who are heterosexual? They feel at home here too. The reason both the gay couples and straight couples can sit on the same pew and look to God is that I don't make sexual orientation an issue."

I'm pressured all the time to take positions, but I steadfastly refuse. Every person has a right to sit on the pew: Republicans and Democrats, libertarians and anarchists, pro-choice and pro-life, gay and straight.

I speak out against injustice, but I refuse to take political positions that offend people and exclude them from the pew.

I speak out against injustice, but I refuse to take political positions that offend people and exclude them from the pew. Not long ago, someone asked me if I'm an evangelical. My first response was, "No!" After we talked a while, he realized I am a theological evangelical, but not a political evangelical. In America today, the distinction has been blurred so that most people think Pat Robertson and Jerry Falwell's politics represent the evangelical position. They don't—not for me, at least. If Jesus was so careful not to align Himself with political positions, it seems strange that Christian leaders today would be so passionately and dogmatically political. A lot of pastors love the power they receive by taking political stands. It's easy to fan emotional flames and enjoy popularity, but I won't speak up unless I see genuine injustice when "the least of these" are at peril. That's my passion and my responsibility.

- *We teach the truth of God's Word without specific litmus tests of theology.*

If you've read much of this book, you know how much I treasure God's Word. It is my lamp and my sword. It reveals the heart of God and His purposes to bring people out of darkness into His light. But I'm not going to get into fights over specific interpretations of minor points of theology. There are far more important things for me to do than fight those fights. We teach God's Word and help people apply it to their deepest needs and greatest hopes. To be honest, I couldn't care less whether another pastor or writer is a Wesleyan or a Calvinist; pretrib, midtrib, posttrib, or no-trib. I don't care which denomination someone comes from. All I care about is that we pursue Jesus together, marvel at Him for rescuing us from hell by His death for us on the cross, love God with all our hearts, and let His love flow through us as we love our neighbors as ourselves.

> *At the end of the day, people want to know that God is big enough and loving enough to reach into their deepest needs and change their lives. My whole theology boils down to the greatness and the grace of God.*

When I hear someone browbeating someone else about an obscure theological position, it breaks my heart. Yes, there are those who don't value God's Word. That's not an obscure position! And on the other end, I know people who defend the authority of the Bible with such anger that it scares me. Why are they so defensive about grace and truth? That doesn't make sense to me, but they are threatened down to the core of their souls. My fight isn't against another believer who has a slightly different interpretation than mine. My real struggle is against the forces of darkness that imprison men and women who need to be freed by the love and forgiveness of Jesus Christ.

At the end of the day, people want to know that God is big enough and loving enough to reach into their deepest needs and change their lives. My whole theology boils down to the greatness and the grace of God. He is worthy of our trust, no matter what we've done and who we are. God's Word is His message to us about His majesty and kindness. In the pages of the Bible, we learn true humility because Jesus modeled it for us; we find the cleansing power of forgiveness because Jesus paid the price for our sins; and we learn to take initiative to reach out to people to touch them with His love. Without the truth of the Bible, we have no way to know who God really is. As believers soak up God's truth and love people with His incredible love, we become a manifestation of God's grace. That's our role. That's our privilege.

- ### *We examine what the institutionalized church is doing, and we do the opposite.*

At the end of the day, we are radically committed to being different, not just to be different, but to be absolutely sure we stay real and avoid becoming a dead bureaucracy. As a general rule, we watch what most churches are doing, and we do the opposite. When people come to St. John's, they often remark, "Man, I've never seen anything like this before! I wonder why other churches don't do church this way." That's the response people had to Jesus: they were amazed that He wasn't at all like the Pharisees and Sadducees. And that's the response we want them to have when they experience St. John's.

THE DANGER ZONE

It's a challenge to stay fresh and real. If I think too much about what I want instead of what God wants, my selfishness leads me to use people instead of loving them. When I speak of God's love but use a person to make me more successful, that's hypocrisy. When I'm more concerned about making worship good theater instead of trusting the power of God to change lives through our worship, I'm not authentic. When I think too much about what I'm wearing on Sunday morning, or when I am afraid to tell people what's really going on in my life, I'm being less than genuine. When I alter what God wants me to say because I'm concerned about what people will think of me, I've become a fraud.

Authenticity is crucial. In fact, it's an essential ingredient for a relationship built on trust. When someone tells me, "Rudy, I love you," I look into that person's eyes to see if the look matches the words. That's not paranoia; it's human nature to evaluate the trustworthiness of another person. Trust isn't an instantaneous, all-or-nothing thing. It is built brick by brick over many interactions. Trust grows or diminishes according to our perceptions of the person's authenticity. We

God has given me the gift of discernment, so I can usually spot a fake a mile away. I hate it when I look in the mirror and find one. That really stinks.

come to each interaction with a set of unspoken, and probably unknown, expectations about what that person should think about the topic of conversation . . . or about us. In some cases, our expectations are relatively accurate, and they help us relate to that person appropriately, trusting authenticity or distrusting fakery. But in many cases, our expectations are based only on the exterior, and we miss the person's heart completely. We are wise to withhold judgment until we've asked more questions, listened a lot, and learned the truth that may not have been obvious at first.

God has given me the gift of discernment, so I can usually spot a fake a mile away. I hate it when I look in the mirror and find one. That really stinks. God has given me a sharp sense of the boundary between the authentic and the phony, and I know deep in my soul that God loves "a humble and contrite heart." But all kinds of pressures threaten to push me away from genuine love to manipulation for selfish gain. Pastors compare the size of their churches, the significance of their sacrifice, and all kinds of other measuring sticks. My human nature wants to say, "Hey, look at me! I'm doing the job—for Jesus!" But if I'm calling attention to myself, it's not for Jesus. In his second letter to the Corinthians, Paul made an astounding statement. That dude was tough. Nothing got him off track, but he said there was one thing he feared. He wrote, "I am afraid that just as Eve was deceived by the serpent's cunning, your minds may somehow be led astray from your sincere and pure devotion to Christ" (11:3 NIV). Did you get that? Paul was afraid that people (like you and me) would be turned away from a sincere and pure devotion to Christ. What could do that? Satan's temptation to Eve was that she could "be like God," having full control and power. When I think I can have (and deserve to have) power and popularity, I can feel myself slipping away from a sincere and pure devotion to Jesus. That's the danger zone of hypocrisy.

Some people might say, "Rudy, you're a pastor. You shouldn't have those kinds of selfish thoughts. You should be better than that." When I became a pastor, I didn't stop being human. In fact, as a pastor, I need to be even more aware of temptations and sinful desires. If I'm aware of them, I can do something about them. If I try to make people think I'm "above all that," I'm lying to them, and I dishonor God by my lack of authenticity. No, I'm well aware that I'm a sinner, a man who desperately needs God's love, forgiveness, and strength all day every day. I'm on the road, but I haven't arrived. And I won't arrive as long as I'm above ground. I need God's grace all day every day, and I feel very comfortable admitting that fact.

HANDLING OPPOSITION

In Jesus' day, people voted their preference by coming to hear Him or walking away. They vote the same way in our church today. Actually, they vote in two ways: with their wallets and with their feet. If they like what we're doing, they give and they come. If they don't like it, they stop giving and they stop coming. That seems like a simple observation, but we have to be realistic. If the well-to-do don't like our inclusion of the outcasts, they stop supporting our ministry. Our ministry of inclusion and acceptance has cost us a lot, but it cost Jesus much more.

I realized that when a person feels uncomfortable with our inclusion and stops giving and stops coming, God is simply making room for somebody else who desperately needs to feel the raw, unvarnished, incredible love of God.

Is it worth it? Absolutely! When I see the looks on people's faces at the moment they feel loved, it's a thrill. When we cheer someone's anniversary of sobriety, I get excited, because I know what it took to get to that milestone. When I see people in our church reach out to touch (figuratively and literally) smelly, tough, or hopeless people, nothing gives me more joy. But some people don't feel that joy, so they leave. As I watched this happen a few times, I realized that when a person feels uncomfortable with our inclusion and stops giving and stops coming, God is simply making room for somebody else who desperately needs to feel the raw, unvarnished, incredible love of God. We have three services each Sunday, and to be honest, we don't have much room left. When someone leaves because he doesn't feel comfortable with our arms-wide-open inclusion of all people, a needy person soon comes to fill that place.

I appreciate the ministry of negative, exclusive people in my life. No, I'm not being sarcastic. I really do. Over the years, their questions and comments have forced me to think more deeply, pray more fervently, and come to clearer convictions about God's calling for me and for our church. God has used these people to sharpen me and clarify the defining principle of my life and ministry. Thanks to them, our commitment to God's radical love and acceptance has become the driving force of our ministry, the ethos of our community, and the reason people invite their friends to come to our church. More than anything in the world, I want God to use our church and me to touch every person who longs for love. I am forever grateful for the way God has used critical, exclusive people to shape my thinking and clarify my commitments.

We naturally put a lot of stock in the *horizontal* relationships in life. After all, we can see and touch the people around us, and we get immediate feedback of our efforts to love them. But everybody, Christian and non-Christian, loves people who will love them back. At the end of the day, our higher calling is to fulfill the expectations of our *vertical* relationship, our connection with God, so that He looks at us and says, "Yeah, that's what I'm talking about!" I guess I have a pretty simple philosophy of life. I believe that Jesus Christ came to show the love of God to all people—the apparently powerful and the admittedly powerless—but after His ascension into heaven on that hillside two thousand years ago, His Spirit began to operate in the hearts of His people so that we could become His mouth to speak grace and truth, His ears to listen to others' hopes and fears, His eyes to notice needs, His feet to go to them, and His hands to touch them with His care. When we show this love to people who have the capacity to love us back, that's fine, but it's really no big deal. When we love the unlovely, expecting nothing in return, we touch the heart of God, and He smiles at us.

We are, though, real people who live in the real world. By nature, we are selfish. When we commit ourselves to selfless love, we experience tension in our hearts that cries, "Look out for yourself! Don't let anybody take advantage of you!" In those moments (and there are many), we can give up because we've concluded that it's too hard to really love people, or we can dig deeper into the character of our gracious and powerful God. The struggle to do right things for right reasons is both risk and reward. It threatens to get us off track and causes us to live in fear and crave safety, but those very threats drive us to the heart of God so we can experience His grace more fully. As we experience His grace more deeply, paranoia turns into peace, comparison turns into contentment, and jealousy turns into joy. That's keeping it real.

A TOUCHING STORY: STEVEN WIEMAN

Steven Wieman looked as though he was leading a glamorous life—traveling the world as a geologist, prospecting for oil, meeting new people, visiting historic churches. His experiences in these churches, however, left a sour taste in his mouth. He told me, "I was tired of hearing the same old messages. They seemed empty, and I felt jaded about religion."

He had given up on God.

After Steven moved to Houston, a friend invited him to St. John's. He was reluctant to try church again, but the friend insisted. When he came, he felt the wonderful love our church had for him, but Steven was suspicious. He remembers, "I had never felt that kind of love in any other church anywhere in the world, so I thought the love I felt at St. John's couldn't possibly be real." He was willing, though, to come a few more times as a test to see if the love he felt was real or fake. He recalls, "After coming to St. John's a few more weeks, I realized that not only *the love* is real, but *the people* are real too."

Steven had studied the Bible, enough to know what love should look like. He told me, "The love I sensed at St. John's is the *agape* love the Bible talks about . . . unconditional love . . . love that knows no boundaries."

After attending St. John's for about six months, Steven realized that it wasn't just his friend who had brought him to the church. God Himself had brought him there to soak up the love God wanted him to enjoy. No longer would he just *go* to church—now he would *experience* church.

Steven plunged into relationships at St. John's, and he found that people really cared for him. With obvious appreciation, he remembers, "At St. John's I didn't find just an 'extended family.' I found a real family based on love, trust, and mutual respect, and I wouldn't change that for the world."

CHAPTER 9
Intentionally Different

"But woe to you, scribes and Pharisees, hypocrites! For you shut up the kingdom of heaven against men; for you neither go in yourselves, nor do you allow those who are entering to go in." (MATTHEW 23:13 NKJV)

One of the highest of human duties is the duty of encouragement. . . . It is easy to laugh at men's ideals; it is easy to pour cold water on their enthusiasm; it is easy to discourage others. The world is full of discouragers. We have a Christian duty to encourage one another. Many a time a word of praise or thanks or appreciation or cheer has kept a man on his feet. Blessed is the man who speaks such a word. —WILLIAM BARCLAY

Jesus turned the world upside down. People were looking for a political Messiah to set them free from Roman tyranny, but Jesus told them their real need was of the heart. He was the ultimate revolutionary—counterculture to the core. To those considered to be outcasts, He said, "I love you so much I want to hang with you to show you how much I care." To the proud, religious establishment,

He told them, "You're snakes, whitewashed tombs, and you follow your father the devil!" To the powerful Roman governor, He said, "My kingdom is not of this world." To untouchable lepers, He reached out His hand and said, "Come close; I want to touch you and heal you." To overlooked women and children, He gave attention and affection. To those who trusted in their wealth, He told them, "The only stuff that matters is treasure in heaven."

We sometimes think of Jesus as austere and distant or with clenched teeth, fiercely committed to His purpose. Certainly, He was totally committed to His mission to give His life to pay for our sins, but His mood was most often characterized by unmitigated joy. Author and pastor John Piper writes, "But the *glory* and *grace* of Jesus is that he is, and always will be, indestructibly happy. . . . My capacities for joy are very confined. So Christ not only offers himself as the divine object of my joy, but pours his capacity for joy into me, so that I can enjoy him with the very joy of God. This is glory, and this is grace."[1]

I'm continually amazed at Jesus. I can't get over (and I hope I never will get over) His incredible love and purpose for me. His light broke into my darkness, and He brought life into the deadness of my heart. His grace has given me new hope and a new reason to live. Jesus has given me a mandate to touch the life of every person—from the rich and powerful to "the least of these"—with His kindness and strength. He reminds me to keep it fresh and avoid the drift toward institutionalized, soul-numbing structure. And He is revealing a ministry philosophy that is different—as intentionally different as He is.

SAFE OR SPONTANEOUS

I love the church because it's the way God touches people to transform them. But to be honest, I get pretty upset about some leaders in the church when they are more concerned about safety and self-promotion than taking the real message of Jesus to every person in their communities. The leaders I'm talking about aren't just pastors. I'm including people who work on a church staff or volunteer in any ministry at their church. All of us need to take a good, hard look at how we live God's calling in our lives. As we look at what Jesus wants us to do, I'm not claiming to have my act together. I'm still learning, still in process, still in need of God's guidance. I often ask myself and my team if we're really touching people's lives. Are we willing to do whatever it takes to touch them, no matter how many traditions we trample, no matter who doesn't like it? That's what Jesus did. The problem I have with some church leaders isn't that they're still in progress; it's that many of them don't even ask the right questions. They seem to be far more committed to being safe than making a difference. With that perspective, they sure aren't going to have a revolutionary impact for Jesus.

Are we willing to do whatever it takes to touch them, no matter how many traditions we trample, no matter who doesn't like it?

Many of us gravitate to safe forms of ministry that make us feel comfortable. We either follow ancient traditions, or we create new ones, but unless we're careful, these practices anesthetize us and rob us of spiritual spontaneity. Before you write me off completely, I want to assure you that I'm not saying all traditions are evil. I'm only saying that we need to work really hard to keep our own hearts fresh with Jesus and let that freshness overflow in our ministry expressions. If we follow traditions, we need to go deeper into their true meaning so they are as fresh to us today as they were the first time they were used by Augustine, Luther, or Wesley.

People who have been to our church probably think that I advocate our style of lively, loud worship for everybody, but that's not true. As I've studied many faith expressions, I've found that any and all of them can be revolutionary if the person leading has one vital quality: rigorous honesty. Leaders who want to be seen as kings create distance between them and their people, but those who see themselves as fellow travelers on the road of seeking God have the greatest impact on people. People thirst for authentic leaders. They want to connect with leaders who share many of their own struggles and joys as they follow Christ. Most people don't respond very positively to a leader who points a finger and says, "You ought to do this or that." But almost all of us are willing to follow someone who says, "Hey, I'm on the road with you. Let's go forward together."

Leaders who want to be seen as kings create distance between them and their people, but those who see themselves as fellow travelers on the road of seeking God have the greatest impact on people.

Self-disclosure and the long, slow process of growth are threatening to some leaders. They prefer the safety of the illusion of their own perfection, but that illusion creates false expectations in the hearts of their followers. And ultimately, it clouds their faith instead of crystallizing it. A leader's spontaneous, rich, real walk with God is incredibly attractive, it builds trust, and it is a powerful model for people to follow.

Authenticity and transparency are related, but they aren't the same thing. When I first met a friend of mine, he impressed me as an authentic person. I could tell that he was speaking the truth, but he wasn't immediately transparent to tell me all the truth about himself. That's understandable. In the corporate world, people are penalized (or at least are suspect) if they are too open too soon with too many people. As I got to know this friend, he gradually told me stories about his background, his wounds, and his hopes and fears. In a strong leader, appropriate self-disclosure is essential. It tells people this leader can be trusted to come alongside and walk the journey with them instead of using and manipulating them for personal gain. Authenticity builds trust; transparency builds intimacy.

Why do so many church leaders gravitate toward safety? There are probably many reasons, but one of them is that they often measure the wrong things. They measure the observable instead of the hidden, the size of attendance or the budget instead of the work of the Spirit. Fear drives many of us to want to be seen as successful, not failures, as popular instead of rejected—or worse, ignored. Above all, we want to be safe. If we succeed, we want the credit, and if we fail, we want to be able to blame our traditions or other people. We may also gravitate toward safety because we're simply too stressed and tired to be creative and try something new. Maybe we've tried a new idea in the past, and it failed and we got blasted. That experience taught us to crawl into our shells and not take any more "dumb risks." But that's the wrong lesson. Jesus put Himself at risk day after day in every situation. His only measurement was fulfilling the Father's will, and He was willing to do whatever it took to accomplish that purpose. He was often misunderstood, even by those closest to Him, but nothing stopped Him from focusing on the ultimate measurement: the approval of the Father.

A leader's spontaneous, rich, real walk with God is incredibly attractive, it builds trust, and it is a powerful model for people to follow.

At St. John's, we try very hard to measure the right things. Of course, we measure attendance and the budget, but that's *not all* we measure, and it's *not primarily* what we measure. We celebrate individuals taking steps of faith, no matter who that person is or how haltingly the step was taken. We look not only at the number of volunteers who serve in our ministries, but the looks on their faces. If they're thrilled to be serving God and helping people, we're on the right track. But when they serve primarily out of guilt or obligation, we've got some work to do to bring the fresh air of grace-filled motivation. I'm thrilled that our numbers have grown and the budget is bigger, but we look much more closely for the Spirit's work in individual lives to bring light out of darkness and create joy instead of guilt.

Almost all commentators who look at the church today observe that the denominations and churches that are committed to active, cutting-edge evangelism are the ones that are actually growing. They don't just have an accurate, biblical *theology* of justification by faith; their beliefs translate into *action*. They are actively involved in reaching the lost with the saving message of Jesus. In fact, it's in their organizational DNA. They talk often about the needs of the lost, and they equip their people to touch their neighbors with the gospel. These churches aren't afraid to tell people (as Jesus told them so often) that hell is just as real as heaven. It's a place of eternal torment, where the "worm does not die, and the fire is not quenched" (Mark 9:48 NIV). With a sense of urgency, these churches tailor their goals and plans to be sure lost people hear the message, sense the love, and feel welcome. But in the most effective of these churches, evangelism isn't just proclaiming a message, it's building relationships. Paul expressed this idea in one of his letters when he wrote: "So, affectionately longing for you, we were well pleased to impart to you not only the gospel of God, but also our own lives, because you [have] become dear to us" (1 Thess. 2:8 NKJV). When we hear about people getting saved, those aren't just notches in our evangelistic gun belts. Those are real people with

> *We look not only at the number of volunteers who serve in our ministries, but the looks on their faces. If they're thrilled to be serving God and helping people, we're on the right track.*

real hurts and hopes. They aren't targets or goals. In Paul's life, compassion and urgency blended and came to a boiling point of zeal. In his letter to the Romans, he wrote that if he could, he'd go to hell if it meant lost people he loved would come to Christ. That's passion!

When I hear of someone turning from sin to salvation, I remember two things: that the angels are having a party to celebrate, and that the person's life, now and forever, has been rescued and changed by the grace of God.

When I hear of someone turning from sin to salvation, I remember two things: that the angels are having a party to celebrate, and that the person's life, now and forever, has been rescued and changed by the grace of God. Each person is far more than a statistic. Each one represents the intentional work of God to touch a life.

Today, perhaps more than ever, people are looking for authenticity in churches. That fact is evident in their response to the gospel. Donald Miller, the author of *Blue Like Jazz*, has become a respected critic of American church culture. Earlier in his life, he felt disillusioned by most churches he attended. He wrote:

> I felt like people were trying to sell me Jesus. I was salesman for a while, and we were taught that you are supposed to point out all the benefits of a product when you are selling it. That is how I felt about some of the preachers I heard speak. They were always pointing out the benefits of the Christian faith. That rubbed me wrong. It's not that there aren't benefits, there are, but did they have to talk about spirituality like it's a vacuum cleaner?[2]

Later, Miller found a church and a pastor he really liked. He explained the difference: "I didn't want to befriend somebody just to trick them into going to my church. Rick [the pastor] said that was not what he was talking about. He said he was talking about loving people just because they exist—homeless people and Gothic people and gays and fruit nuts. And then I liked the sound of it."[3] That's what I'm talking about too.

CULTURAL CONTEXT

The church can learn a lot from Oprah, Dr. Phil, and reality television. In the past thirty years, the culture has changed. Years ago, people who came to church expected a prescribed set of activities and rituals that made them feel comfortable. Today, we live in the Media Age, and people spend much more time watching *Oprah* and reality TV shows. These programs are personal, fast-paced, and full of drama. That's our classroom (and in some ways, our competition), and understanding that fact helps us construct our worship services in a way that is lively, spontaneous, and gritty. If people feel touched, they'll laugh and cry, applaud and yell, wince and sigh. Maybe they'll even want to attend more often.

From my reading of the Gospels, that's how it seems that people responded to Jesus. They had the opportunity to respond in that way because Jesus went out to be among them. He didn't stay in Jerusalem and write memos from His office. The gospels show Him among common people and leaders, Jews and ethnic outcasts, in cities and in the country, wherever people lived. In all those places and at all those times, He touched them. In the same way, I want people who come to St. John's to connect with Jesus and His people in ways that touch their hearts.

Far too often, ministries today are known for one thing: it may be great worship, terrific teaching, innovative outreach, social action, effective groups, or a beautiful building. But in their focus on only one thing, they separate spiritual growth from meeting physical needs of people (if they are involved in meeting physical needs at all). In *Walking with the Poor,* Bryant Myers asserts that the two-tiered

This connection emphasizes the inseparable nature of spiritual and physical needs in the Gospels.

approach to the world is a "false dichotomy that separates evangelism as spiritual activity of the church from the social action of the physical realm."[4] In the passage referred to so often in these pages, Jesus combines the meeting of physical needs of "the least of these" with our spiritual motivation to honor Jesus. This connection emphasizes the inseparable nature of spiritual and physical needs in the Gospels.

Is the life and ministry of Jesus an unattainable ideal for us? No, only weeks after Jesus ascended back to heaven, we find the fledgling group of believers in Jerusalem meeting physical and spiritual needs. Luke tells us:

> They continued steadfastly in the apostles' doctrine and fellowship, in the breaking of bread, and in prayers. Then fear came upon every soul, and many wonders and signs were done through the apostles. Now all who believed were together, and had all things in common, and sold their possessions and goods, and divided them among all, as anyone had need. So continuing daily with one accord in the temple, and breaking bread from house to house, they ate their food with gladness and simplicity of heart, praising God and having favor with all the people. And the Lord added to the church daily those who were being saved. (Acts 2:42–47 NKJV).

Do you see the power of meeting both physical and spiritual needs in the earliest moments of the church's life? That's the

We tend to stay stuck in our routines until something jars us out of our ruts.

model for our ministry here at St. John's too.

Escaping the cocoon of safety and pursuing a cutting-edge ministry of meeting a variety of needs doesn't just happen. We tend to stay stuck in our routines until something jars us out of our ruts. Some of us are shaken by a trip to Guatemala or Haiti or Liberia, where we see desperate physical and spiritual needs, and we're compelled to help anyone we can help, there or back at home. And some of us are jarred awake by a tragedy in our own lives. As we experience God's touch through others, we want to touch people too. Some of us look with fresh eyes at the life of Jesus, and we realize we've only been playing at our faith. It's time to get real. There may be a thousand triggers to propel us out of our safety zone, but the important thing is that we come to grips with reality and get moving.

A QUICK LOOK

As we've seen, movements of the Spirit started with a fresh vision of God and His calling, an honest appraisal of needs, and zeal to touch people's lives. In the early stages, these movements were spontaneous and fully alive. As they aged, however, many of them moved from being "intentionally spontaneous" to "intentionally safe." Let's take a quick glance at some differences between the two.

- *Ministries that are intentionally safe . . .*
  - measure and celebrate size of attendance and budgets

  - use traditions without much reflection

  - resist change and avoid failure at all costs

- focus resources on insiders

- value stability

- often project the leader as perfect (or close to it)

- avoid risks and value organizational survival

- develop their own language for insiders

- see the leader's role as a CEO who controls almost everything with centralized planning and decision making

- become a fortress to protect people from the world

- normalize risk avoidance and make safety the ethic

- are protective of facilities

- are threatened by those who ask hard questions

- *Ministries that are intentionally spontaneous . . .*
  - measure and celebrate intangibles of zeal, love, and spiritual vitality

  - may use traditions, but often explain the real meaning

  - embrace change

  - focus resources on both community impact and member growth

  - value creativity and are willing to learn from failure

  - select leaders who are transparent, authentic, and honest

  - take reasonable risks to make a difference

  - use plain English and avoid insider language

- see the leader's role as the primary vision caster who expects much of the planning to be done at the grass-roots level

- become a welcoming family

- normalize spontaneity, freshness, and love

- are willing to use facilities to the max to make people feel comfortable

- regularly ask hard questions about purpose, scope, and effectiveness

Traditionalists, by their nature, look to the past for answers for the future. They do things this way because they've always done them this way. I'm not an anarchist (though I've been accused of being one), but I feel very sad when I see churches that aren't touching their communities because they are so inwardly focused, bogged down by their insistence on safety and fear of taking risks.

Our culture values immediacy, personal connection, and experience. That's what Oprah and Dr. Phil give to people, and that's what they subconsciously look for in their church experiences.

Our culture values immediacy, personal connection, and experience. That's what Oprah and Dr. Phil give to people, and that's what they subconsciously look for in their church experiences. If traditions can be refreshed so they provide a powerful experience of God's character and presence, then by all means use them. But don't forfeit your God-given opportunity to touch the lives of hurting people all around you because you are too frightened or burned out to take a risk to reach out to them.

CHOICES TO MAKE

In the opening pages of his insightful book, *Good to Great*, author Jim Collins observes that organizations (such as schools, churches, and businesses) usually are quite satisfied with being good enough. If they were truly bad, someone would do something about it. He writes:

> We don't have great schools, principally because we have good schools. We don't have great government, principally because we have good government. Few people attain great lives, in large part because it is just so easy to settle for a good life. The vast majority of companies [or churches] never become great, precisely because the vast majority become quite good—and that is their main problem.[5]

Collins and his research staff examined thousands of companies, and they identified eleven that made the difficult transition from "good to great." Here are some of the surprising observations that surfaced:

○ Charismatic leaders brought in from the outside to fix the organization often hindered progress.

○ Clarity of vision, not just the presence of a strategic plan, propelled change.

○ They didn't focus only on what to do to become great. They focused equally on what *not* to do and what to *stop* doing.

○ Technology isn't a substitute for vision. It can accelerate change, but it can't ignite it.

○ They didn't have a launch event or snappy marketing theme for the change. They simply made changes in perspective, purpose, and perhaps, in personnel, and the changes happened.

○ Many of them succeeded incredibly well even in depressed industries. "Greatness," Collins asserts, "is not a function of circumstance. Greatness, it turns out, is largely a matter of conscious choice."[6]

Conscious choice. That's what I'm advocating—conscious choices to ask hard questions, be brutally honest, commit to change, and muster the courage to take action. Without this process, we'll stay stuck having good enough ministries that touch enough lives in good enough ways so that we're satisfied and complacent. When I read the Gospels and Acts, I don't see people who were satisfied with "good enough." Jesus modeled, and the disciples eventually followed, the example of selfless humility and radical activism. The mandate Jesus gave His men was to reach the entire globe, and His sacrifice fueled their zeal.

When I read the Gospels and Acts, I don't see people who were satisfied with "good enough." Jesus modeled, and the disciples eventually followed, the example of selfless humility and radical activism.

WARMTH AND AUTHENTICITY

Grand plans and intense zeal are great, but they don't necessarily touch lives. We have to get out and among the people. We have to minister "with" our communities so that we know people's names and ask about their hopes and fears. Ultimately, we only touch lives if we build friendships with people, whether they know Christ or not, whether they come to our church or not, or whether they repay our kindness or not. The men and women at St. John's who really make a difference are those who connect with people this way. They may be leaders of a ministry, volunteers in the nursery, or just members of our church family. Each of these people, though, is an ambassador—not to a nation, but to a name: individuals they see from day to day, people Jesus loves to death, people who have intrinsic value as human beings created in the image of God. Friendships are the power of ministry. I'm just a guy with a smile on my face, passing a piece of bread and a bowl of soup to a friend.

Earlier I defined the difference between ministering "to" a community, "in" a community, and "with" a com-

Friendships are the power of ministry.

munity. We may send resources to people in need. That's fine, but it doesn't build close friendships. A ministry "in" a community has a fortress mentality, in which the church sees itself protecting its people from the evil, dirt, sickness, and needs around them. Until people in a church see themselves as a vital part of their community—their whole community—they won't assertively and consciously build friendships with every person of every economic level, every color, every lifestyle, and every smell. Self-protection, the *fear* of losing our sense of safety, effectively closes our eyes to the needs of others and rivets our attention on ourselves. Our God-given purpose is to soak in the love of God so deeply that "the love of Christ controls us . . . [and we] no longer live for ourselves but for Him who died and rose again on our behalf" (2 Cor. 5:15). When that happens, we won't worry as much about the risks. If our *faith* in Jesus is rich, fresh, and real, we'll be glad to "lose our lives" as His love overflows from our hearts.

When I walk into a church, I can tell almost immediately if the leader is authentic, transparent, and warm. If he is, the entire congregation exudes these qualities. It's almost palpable. People greet me warmly, and there's a vibrant sense of life in the air. If, though, the leader values safety over spontaneity, I sense that people don't really know what's expected of them. They follow the prescribed rituals of the church, but they seem empty, stiff, and lifeless. In those churches, people may greet me, but it sometimes seems perfunctory, as though they've read in a job description that they're supposed to smile and extend a hand to greeters. Man, I can't wait to get out of those places!

A friend of mine told me that he went to one of these churches for several years. The congregation mirrored the pastor's stiff demeanor. He talked every week about their church being a family, but my friend realized that it followed the rules of a dysfunctional family: don't feel, don't talk, don't trust. It was acceptable for people to feel joy and praise God, but if they expressed sadness or anger, people tried to "fix" them. They could talk about anything in the world, except they weren't allowed to question the pastor's decisions. And in that environment, people were constantly playing games with each other, competing with each other to see who could keep from getting hurt and who could come out on top. They tried to control others' behav-

They tried to control others' behavior, but control is a poor substitute for trust.

ior, but control is a poor substitute for trust. That church's ministry is well-planned and ordered, but it's lifeless. Over the years, however, people have learned to not expect anything else. My friend eventually decided to leave that church and look for one that had more life.

Most pastors and other leaders who are stiff and distant aren't that way because they're evil people. In the vast majority of cases, they are good-hearted people who really want to please God, but they are following the only ministry model they've ever seen: wearing masks and playing roles. They live according to what the seminary, the denomination, or their mentor told them they *should* be. But the mask of the completely competent, always-in-control, never-bothered leader hides the real, flesh-and-blood person who, no matter how spiritually mature he or she may be, struggles with the pain, complexity, and fears of being human. The mask tells people, "I'm okay. Don't mess with me. You may need me, but I don't need you." The mask has the look of authority and power—and distance. An emphasis on excellence instead of intimacy and integrity allows the leader to continue to hide.

Hiding comes naturally to fallen people like you and me. Before they sinned, Adam and Eve were "naked" and "not ashamed" (Gen. 2:25 NKJV). They enjoyed being the people God created them to be, without a hint of defensiveness or bitterness or competition. As soon as they sinned, though, they immediately felt ashamed and covered themselves. We've been doing it ever since. It's part of the human condition to feel compelled to cover up our inadequacies and project an image of power and control. We've just moved the fig leaves up to mask our faces.

It's part of the human condition to feel compelled to cover up our inadequacies and project an image of power and control. We've just moved the fig leaves up to mask our faces.

A person who has the courage to take off the mask becomes a real person taking real risks in relationships. Trust is more important than control; warmth is a higher priority than excellence. This leader still wants to do things well, but competence is a means to the end of pleasing God and touching hearts, not a way to prove his worth. The authentic leader is willing to share some struggles and hurts, and people feel connected to him. He has authority, but he doesn't use it to reign over people. He realizes he is flawed, and he uses his authority as a leader to serve. He knows very well that he isn't perfect, and he tells people often that he's on the road of growth—just like they are. He celebrates others' successes even more than his own.

Does all this sound strange . . . even wrong? I feel comfortable with my encouragement to leaders to be transparent, because I've been looking at God's Word, and I find lots of examples there. Look at the Psalms. David was the king of Israel, and he could have easily hidden his hopes, hurts, and fears, but he didn't. His poems depict—clearly and permanently—his highest hopes and deepest depression, his intense fears and his greatest praise for God. David hung it all out for us to see! And Paul, the first and foremost missionary of our faith, admitted, "For what I am doing, I do not understand. For what I will to do, that I do not practice; but what I hate, that I do" (Rom. 7:15 NKJV). Hey, that sounds like me! And he confided that he still had a long way to go in his walk with Jesus. He wrote, "Not that I

I don't see myself as a CEO at St. John's. I'm more of a gang leader.

have already attained, or am already perfected; but I press on, that I may lay hold of that for which Christ Jesus has also laid hold of me" (Phil. 3:12 NKJV). These leaders—two of the strongest, most effective leaders the world has ever known—were honest about their struggles. They are my examples, and they are yours, too.

I learned a lot from the recovery community about being transparent. Step 1 is admitting our sins, wounds, and destructive behavior. Step 4 requires us to take a "searching and fearless moral inventory" to identify harmful attitudes and actions so we can repent, and Step 5 challenges us to admit our faults to God, ourselves, and another person. I don't expect everybody to go to the extremes I am willing to go to in my leadership style, but maybe it would be helpful to share a few commitments I've made to be authentic, transparent, and trustworthy:

- I often tell the congregation or individuals what I'm struggling with that day—not after I've resolved and sugarcoated it.

- I have no secrets, except those others have shared with me about themselves.

- My wounds are visible to all. Some of my hurts have healed and scarred over, but a few are still open and bleeding. I tell people the unvarnished truth.

- I don't see myself as a CEO at St. John's. I'm more of a gang leader.

- There's no doubt that I'm still in process. I don't expect perfection in this life, only step-by-step progress by the grace of God.

- I never talk about a topic unless I've experienced it myself.

- I speak the brutal truth to others, and I expect them to speak it to me. My dad used to say, "It's a whole lot easier to tell the truth, because you don't have to remember what you said."

- When I mess up (which is often), I try to admit it to God and to the people I offended as quickly as possible, no matter how embarrassing it may be.

If you are a pastor, I sincerely believe that God is calling you to take off any mask you might be wearing to protect yourself, and He wants you to be an authentic leader. He's asking you to do what I do quite often: go to God with an honest heart and pray, "Lord Jesus, show me if I'm wearing a mask, and help me be more authentic, transparent, and warm." Wearing or taking off a mask isn't a game.

It's serious business. The mask is designed to win approval and protect us from rejection. The Pharisees were doing the same thing, and Jesus told them bluntly, "You are the ones who justify yourselves in the eyes of men, but God knows your hearts. What is highly valued among men is detestable in God's sight" (Luke 16:15 NIV). Have the courage to be painfully honest with God about trying to justify yourself before men by wearing a mask. And repent. Pour out your heart to Him, and let His wonderful, unconditional love touch the deepest recesses of your soul. As you feel increasingly secure in His loving hands, you'll be able to resist the temptation to put that mask on again.

Taking the mask off and being real is risky, but it offers the hope of loving and being loved for who you are, of touching others and being touched.

If people instantly appreciate your new honesty, that's fantastic. If they don't, at least you're pleasing the One who called you. But realize that if you've been wearing a mask and playing a role for a long time, you probably have a lot of people around you who are playing roles too. When you change, they might feel tremendously threatened—until they realize your change is real. Taking the mask off and being real is risky, but it offers the hope of loving and being loved for who you are, of touching others and being touched. First, take the mask off with God and yourself, and then find at least one other person who will encourage you to be painfully honest.

If you're a staff member, volunteer, or church member, don't jump to blame your pastor for being inauthentic. He's probably doing the best he knows how to do. Start with your own heart. Ask God for clarity and courage to take your mask off so you can be more authentic. As you become more transparent and trustworthy, you can be a beacon of light to the people around you. And who knows? God might even use you to bring a revolution of love in your family, your church, and your community. Wouldn't that be fantastic? Jesus told a parable about a mustard seed, the smallest seed known to them (Mark 4:30–32). When the tiny seed took root, it grew into one of the largest bushes in the garden. Our efforts to bring the refreshment of God's love to every person in the community may begin on a very small scale, but eventually, God will produce some remarkable growth. Don't minimize your own impact for God. He may use you in ways you never imagined!

And pray for me. I need God's help, because I still have a long way to go.

The church is God with skin on. It's how He has chosen to accomplish His purpose to touch every person with His love. The great preacher D. L. Moody accurately observed, "Out of one hundred men, one will read the Bible; the other ninety-nine will read the Christian." People are looking for authenticity. Let's not let them down.

A TOUCHING STORY: MARGO HARRIS

By the time Margo came to St. John's, she had been in recovery for about ten years. She had gone to church when she was a child, and she realized she needed to start going to church again. Margo visited Windsor Village a number of times, and she heard Pastor Caldwell encouraging people to attend a new church across town: St. John's. She decided to try it out the next Sunday. She told me, "As soon as I walked through the doors at St. John's, I felt a warm, wonderful presence. I knew I was home. At the door people greeted me with hugs. I didn't feel that I had to act a certain way to be accepted. To be honest, I'd always been intimidated by church folks because I thought they expected me to act a certain way, but at St. John's, it was different: I immediately felt loved and accepted. It hit me that this must be the way God wants people to feel when they come to church. That was the first day, and I've never left the love I found at St. John's."

Years before, Margo had been one of the first black women involved in Cocaine Anonymous. She and a friend in the group realized that a lot of black people who were cocaine addicts were attending Alcoholics Anonymous meetings, so they started their own group and invited other addicts to come. Soon, the group swelled into a movement of people in CA recovery. When Margo started attending St. John's, dozens of these people in recovery followed her to the church. Actually, Margo didn't even realize so many people were following her to church, but I noticed that a lot of new people were coming to St. John's because they were following Margo, her friend, and a couple of other CA leaders. Margo told me, "When all these people came to St. John's, they felt the same way I felt when I first came here. They'd never felt loved like this before! And they stayed too."

A friend asked Margo, "How did God touch your life at St. John's?"

She replied, "That first Sunday, I was hungry for truth. That morning, Rudy showed so much love to every person who walked in the door, and Juanita preached God's Word in an incredibly powerful way. Love and truth: that's what changed my life."

Not long after Margo came to St. John's, she started spending time with Juanita. Margo remembers that time: "I saw peace and joy in Juanita's life that I'd never seen in anyone before. She depended totally on God. I had depended on *anything* and *anyone* but God, so Juanita's example made me really hungry to trust God like she did."

Juanita started a Bible study and invited Margo and several other women. As they spent time together in the Word, Margo learned to trust God more than ever before, and she learned about the power and presence of the Holy Spirit. "I'd heard a lot about Jesus and the Father," Margo related to a friend, "but I'd never known much about the Holy Spirit. I began to study the Word and watch Pastor Rudy and Pastor Juanita's example. Whenever anything came up, they always said, 'Let's pray about that.' Their lives and their faith were so attractive and full of God's Spirit, and I wanted to be like them. The transformation I experienced was truly being 'born again.'"

Margo had been a successful professional in the world of fashion. She had organized photo shoots and fashion and talent shows for many years, but after being at St. John's for a while, she felt led by God to use her talents for God's kingdom. For the last several years, she has led our worship team. She loves the artistry and beauty of dance, and she has led the dancers who praise God in our worship services. She remembers, "I began to recognize gifts and talents God had given me, but I'd never noticed before. And it was amazing to me that I could dance for the Lord, lead a team of people to bless others, and help people experience the love and power of God's Spirit and God's Word. I never imagined all this could happen to me. I'm so thankful for the way God has used Pastor Rudy and Pastor Juanita in my life."

CHAPTER 10
It's Worth It

*His master said to him, "Well done, good and faithful servant; you have been faithful over a few things, I will make you ruler over many things. Enter into the joy of your master." (*MATTHEW 25:21*)*

I judge all things only by the price they shall gain in eternity.
—JOHN WESLEY

Jesus promised that following Him with all our hearts would bring wonderful blessings as well as painful costs. That's certainly been true in my life. I could never have imagined that God would use me in the lives of others as He has. It's all because of His great grace. But I've experienced loss too. The most bitter and painful wound occurred after I chose to walk away from the family business and my dad told his friends, "I've lost Rudy to God." We had always been so close. I respected him and loved him, but at that moment, it felt as if an ax had severed the bond between us. It hurt. It really hurt. There were times that I wondered if following Jesus was worth all that pain.

FULL CIRCLE

When we began our ministry at St. John's, God poured out His grace and strength to touch many lives. Still, in my heart I felt the nagging loss of my dad. After several years went by, I looked up one Sunday morning and saw my dad taking a seat at church. Man, what a day! For the next six years, he almost never missed a Sunday service. He began to change his perception of me and my choice to follow Jesus, and I heard that he told his friends, "I finally found a preacher I could trust." That was an incredible compliment—Dad had come full circle.

Six years after he started attending St. John's, Dad came forward to receive Christ as his Savior. As you can imagine, no words can describe my joy at seeing my father express his faith in Jesus.

But seven years later, my dad got very sick. Mom, Juanita, and I were with him in the hospital when the doctor came in with the results of tests he had ordered. He stood next to my father's bed and told him plainly, "Mr. Rasmus, we've looked at the tests and your condition. Sir, you are dying. Your heart is diseased, and it's inoperable. I'm sorry."

"Baby, I'm going to live every day like I'm going to live forever."

Dad looked at the doctor and said with calm resignation, "Well, doc, if that's the way it is, then that's the way it is."

After the doctor left the room, Juanita tenderly asked Dad, "How do you feel about the news?"

He smiled at her and said, "Baby, I'm going to live every day like I'm going to live forever."

For the next eight weeks, Dad got the most out of every single day. He never looked worried or afraid. He was confident that God was in complete control. He asked Juanita to write out a particular verse of Scripture, frame it, and bring it to him at the hospital. You have to understand, my father had never been a Bible scholar—not in the least. When I was growing up, I only heard him quote one verse. Before every meal, he solemnly pronounced with a twinkle in his eye, "Rise, Peter. Slay and eat!" But now Dad wanted a constant reminder of God's comfort. The verse he chose is, "The battle is not yours, but the Lord's." His faith impressed me. Dad took that framed verse with him from room to room as he went in and out of the hospital during those weeks.

To Dad, living as if he was "going to live forever" meant that no good-bye was ever final, and he always acted as though he was sure he'd see us again. Until his last day, he kept working, and he kept files of papers piled on his bed so he could stay on top of his work.

His health declined very gradually. One night, the doctors gave him three doses of nitro for his heart, but he didn't seem to be in imminent danger of dying. I stayed with him awhile, and when it was late, I walked to the door and said, "See you later, Dad."

He smiled and told me, "See you, Mr. President." All my life, Dad called me Mr. President, Boss Man, or Big Shot. That night, I was "Mr. President." I smiled at him, walked through the door, and went home.

That night, Dad slipped away. When I found out the next morning, my heart broke with grief, but I also thought about the blessing God had given me to see our fractured relationship restored. I thought about all the years I had known my dad, and I realized what an incredible man he was. He had experienced some tough years, and some of the pain was because of his own decisions. He had always included me in his life and valued me. He trusted me as his friend and his business partner. That's why it hurt him so badly when I chose to follow Jesus and we parted ways for a couple of years. I knew God was real. That's why I responded to Him in faith.

But I was also vividly aware that my faith was costing me dearly: relationally and financially. My dad rejected me, and I found myself with a growing family and my chief source of income gone. I was afraid of losing someone I loved, and that fear became a stark reality. I was also afraid of all the unknowns in the future. I loved adventure, but this didn't feel like an adventure. It felt like a foolish risk.

That, though, is exactly what Jesus calls us to be: foolish—fools for Christ. As I look back today, Jesus' words in Matthew 16 shine in my experience like a neon light: If we pick up our crosses and follow Him, we will certainly "lose" certain things we hold dear. But His promise is that we'll "find" something far more precious (vv. 24–25). That's what God did in my life. When I chose to follow Jesus, I lost the close bond my dad and I had enjoyed as best friends and business partners. There was certainly no guarantee that Dad would come to Christ, but God gave me blessings far more valuable than I could ever imagine. In addition to all the other gifts and blessings God has given me in these years, my father and I have become brothers in Christ, with the promise of an eternity together. That's cool beyond words.

> *In addition to all the other gifts and blessings God has given me in these years, He gave me a relationship with my dad as brothers in Christ, with the promise of an eternity together. That's cool beyond words.*

That insight, though, would come long after the difficult days of my dad's feeling I had betrayed him by following Jesus.

THE RISKS AND REWARDS OF MY CALLING

It may sound schizophrenic, but during the time of upheaval and tension between my dad and me, certainty and fear lived together in my heart. I never questioned the reality of God's touch and the changes He was making in me. The radical shifts in my life from darkness to light and from selfishness to love were beyond doubt, but I didn't choose to go into the ministry as a vocation. God called me to it. It was His idea, His choice, and His leading. In fact, during some difficult periods over the years, I would have left the ministry many times, but I couldn't discount God's clear call for me to be in full-time ministry. Of course, all believers are ministers, but some are called into vocational ministry. I was simply responding in obedience to God's clear, compelling calling.

Even though becoming a pastor wasn't my choice, I am 100 percent, totally invested in what God wants me to be and do. The call stays fresh and real because I often remember where I came from. I had been "the chief of sinners," a sort of "ringmaster in hell," but Jesus touched me and rescued me. I'm also refreshed by seeing God work in the lives of others around me. Every time I hear an addict tell us that he's been sober for a month, a year, or a decade, it thrills my soul. Every time I see a couple that had been torn apart by bitterness now healed and restored by the grace of God, my calling is confirmed. Every time I see hope in the eyes of people who have been hopeless, I am thrilled to take part in God's call to touch them.

> *Every time I see hope in the eyes of people who have been hopeless, I am thrilled to be a little part in God's work to touch them.*

God has given me some wonderful people who have kept me on track. Juanita's love and support is the best thing in my life. There have been plenty of times when I've been down and she's given me a fresh injection of hope in God's sovereignty and goodness. My daughters, Morgan and Ryan, have shown me the power of applying Christian principles in the middle of the forces of popular culture.

Kirbyjon was instrumental in getting me going in ministry, and he continues to be a wonderful friend and mentor. Every week, I pray by phone with four pastors who are scattered across the country, Dred and Andre in Baltimore, Joe in Washington, D.C., and Vance in Nashville. We try to live authentically with each other. Our discussions and prayers each week provide the support and accountability we all need. God has used a host of people to touch me over the years: my mother and father; Auntie Mae Mae; Willie Lane and the men in our Bible study; the pioneers from Windsor Village who helped us get started at St. John's; our staff, board members, and volunteers, who serve out of a "simple and pure devotion" to Jesus; and all the people who have said yes to Jesus in a thousand different ways as we have reached out to them. God has used each one to touch me and shape my life, and I'll never forget them.

As I stay deeply connected with people in need, a constant specter is the risk of burnout. It would be a lot easier if I spent all my time administrating programs and working with only sharp, stable, competent people, but that's not an option. God has called me to connect in deep, meaningful ways with the entire spectrum of our community, but that can be incredibly draining. I have to get away from time to time to regain perspective. If I don't, I risk my family, my ministry, and my sanity. But getting away isn't enough. I have to go deeper and deeper into the heart of God to be refreshed by His love and power. I desperately need to grasp the wonder of His purposes and "know the love of Christ which passes knowledge" (Eph. 3:19 NKJV). Here's the benchmark for me: If my heart isn't filled with wonder, then I'm running on past experience, and I'm at risk for burnout. Sometimes I feel like quitting, which is why I need God to regularly (if not constantly) touch me with the incredible wonder of His grace, His infinite power, and His inscrutable ways. I don't have to have all the answers, and I don't have to have all the clout. I just have to be overwhelmed with amazement that God is who He is—and that I can't provide all that I need. That's enough to keep me going until the next time I'm overwhelmed and feel like quitting.

If my heart isn't filled with wonder, then I'm running on past experience, and I'm at risk for burnout.

Is Jesus overwhelming to you today? I'm encouraged by the story of John, who was probably Jesus' closest friend on earth. At dinner, before Jesus was betrayed, tried, and crucified, John was the disciple who rested his head on Jesus' chest. In his gospel and his letters, John also is the writer who speaks most often and most passionately about the love of Jesus. From these glimpses, we might think John felt pretty comfortable with Jesus. In the opening chapter of Revelation, John tells us about an encounter with the risen Christ. Jesus appeared to him in a vision, and John described the scene:

> Then I turned to see the voice that spoke with me. And having turned I saw seven golden lampstands, and in the midst of the seven lampstands One like the Son of Man, clothed with a garment down to the feet and girded about the chest with a golden band. His head and hair were white like wool, as white as snow, and His eyes like a flame of fire; His feet were like fine brass, as if refined in a furnace, and His voice as the sound of many waters; He had in His right hand seven stars, out of His mouth went a sharp two-edged sword, and His countenance was like the sun shining in its strength. (Rev. 1:12–16 NKJV)

How do you think Jesus' best friend responded to this awesome image? John tells us, "And when I saw Him, I fell at His feet as dead"

(v. 17 NKJV). Blown away. John was blown away when he saw the greatness of Jesus. In fact, he was so overwhelmed that he fainted! But then, said John, "He laid His right hand on me, saying to me, 'Do not be afraid; I am the First and the Last. I am He who lives, and was dead, and behold, I am alive forevermore. Amen. And I have the keys of Hades and of Death'" (vv. 17b–18 NKJV).

When I'm approaching compassion fatigue and burnout, I'm tempted to get mad at Jesus for not doing more to help me. Instead, I need to have a fresh vision of Jesus. If my perception of Him approaches the reality of His incredible greatness, I'll be blown away. That puts a lot of things in perspective!

IN THE MOMENT

For the first two years I was at St. John's, I cried almost every day. The realization of the desperate needs of people got to me. I sensed their hopelessness and helplessness, and I cried for them. I was well aware that only a short time before, my career had been dedicated to destroying lives, and it broke my heart that I had caused such pain. But I also cried because I was also aware that God was now using me to repair some of the damage. I could hardly believe God would use me to restore broken people.

I have to live in the moment.

To stay fresh, I have to be honest, and I have to be real. If I try to put on a mask and act as if nothing bothers me, the repressed emotions will eat me alive. Recently, a friend's mother died. I was touched by her loss, and I cried for a while. It takes a lot out of me to be involved in people's lives. If I try to retreat away from my feelings of sadness, I become completely numb, and I can't experience any emotion, including joy or love.

I have to live in the moment. I can't afford to live in the past and relive either successes or failures, and I can't afford to live in the future and worry about what might happen. The only time I can do anything about is right now. Each moment, God wants to touch me, and each moment, God might use me to touch someone else. If I'm preoccupied with the past or the future, I'll risk missing the beauty of *this* moment God has given me.

Juanita came very close to death in 2001. I emerged from her near-death experience with an unparalleled sense of urgency. I reemerged with clear understanding of the importance of "the moment." There is no one person more important than the one standing in front of me, there is no task more important than the task at hand, and there is no strategic plan that is more important than the pressing problem of that moment. Jesus lived in the moment. No matter what else was going on, He stopped and touched people.

Paradoxically, living in the moment is enhanced when we look at our lives in light of eternity. In the past few months, I've been thinking a lot about Jesus' resurrection and ascension from that hillside back into heaven. Though He is invisible, He's alive—right now, right here, to you and me.

Recently I was talking with some young people about walking with Jesus, and one of them asked me some penetrating questions. After he had listened for a while, he kind of shook his head and said, "Rudy, I don't get it. What difference does it make? How does it affect real stuff in our lives that Jesus lived, died, and came back to life?"

Those are great questions. In fact, I wish everybody asked questions like that. I knew he didn't want a quick, superficial answer, so I thought for a minute, and then I told him, "The difference is that eternity is coming." He smiled and looked at me with a curious expression. I knew I had his attention, so I continued, "Think about athletes. They struggle through long, grueling practices and enjoy the few moments they actually compete in a game, but it's the opposite for us. Our lives today are just practice for eternity, but our lives are incredibly brief in light of the endless, breathtaking, exhilarating game we'll experience for all of eternity. But how we practice in this life will make a huge difference in how we play in eternity. You asked, 'What difference does Jesus make?' He's the one who gets us on the team, who gives us abilities, and who guides us to be the best we can be. Without Him, we just drift around trying to fill our lives with stuff. But with Him, we can learn from our practices here so we'll be ready for all of eternity. The story of Jesus isn't fiction. It's fact. He's alive today, speaking to our hearts, inviting us to join Him and experience more life than we ever thought possible."

Author and pastor Rick Warren wrote, "To make the best use of your life, you must never forget two truths. First, compared with eternity, life is extremely brief. Second, earth is only a temporary residence." Those truths help us live "in the moment" with wisdom, urgency, and hope.

It is an incredible privilege for God to use somebody like me to accomplish His purpose to touch people. It's not a right. I don't deserve this honor. God, in His grace, has given me this wonderful privilege. His willingness to use me certainly isn't because I deserve it due to my pedigree or credentials, and I sure haven't earned it by being flawless. God is willing to use me—even me—*in spite of* who I was, and often *in spite of* who I am. He only asks me to be open to His touch again and again and be available to meet the needs of others. I often remember that Jesus said, "To whom much is given, much is required." I certainly have been given much.

I began my relationship with Jesus by reading the Gospels and looking at how He related to people. Time and time again, He gave people focused attention. He stopped, looked into people's eyes, and reached out to meet their needs. I can easily imagine the look on His face as people responded to His touch with thankfulness, joy, and trust. I can see Him smile. That smile is what I live for every day—when things are going well, and when times are hard; when people are responding positively to my leadership, and when they think I've come from Mars. I love to see God use me to change lives, but I don't live for that. I live for His smile. Over and over again, I think of Jesus' explanation of the reward of following Him: "His master said to him, 'Well done, good and faithful servant; you have been faithful over a few things, I will make you ruler over many things. Enter into the joy of your master'" (Matt. 25:21).

And I can feel his touch.

NOTES

Chapter 1

1. Copyright Christian Washington, used by permission. For more information about this model of change, go to www.realabs.com.

Chapter 2

1. Malcolm Gladwell, *The Tipping Point: How Little Things Can Make a Big Difference* (Back Bay Books, 2002).

Chapter 3

1. Jack Johnson, "The News," *Brushfire Fairytales*, Enjoy Records.
2. *The Journey Home: A Romanian Adoption*, A DLI Productions Film.
3. "Homelessness: Tragic Side Effects of Non-Treatment" (Fact Sheet) (Treatment Advocacy Center, upd. April 2007), www.psychlaws.org/General Resources/fact11.htm.
4. Cited on www.medicinenet.com.
5. Rick Warren, *The Purpose Driven Life*, (Grand Rapids: Zondervan, 2002), 17.
6. Robert C. Linthicum, *Empowering the Poor: Community Organizing Among the City's "Rag, Tag and Bobtail,* (Monrovia, CA: MARC, 1991).
7. Bryant L. Myers, *Walking with the Poor: Principles and Practices of Transformational Development* (Maryknoll, New York: Orbis Books, 1999).
8. Max Lucado, *Just Like Jesus* (Nashville: Word Publishing, 1998), 27–28.

Chapter 4

1. Malcolm Gladwell, *Blink: The Power of Thinking Without Thinking* (New York: Little, Brown, 2005).
2. *The New Testament and Wycliffe Bible Commentary*, (New York: Moody Monthly, The Iverson-Norman Associates, 1971), 31.
3. Richard Swenson, *Margin* (Colorado Springs: Navpress, 1995).

Chapter 5

1. John Piper, *Seeing and Savoring Jesus Christ*, (Wheaton, IL: Crossway Books, 2004), 93–94.
2. Gladwell, *Blink.*
3. Civil Rights Movement Timeline, www.infoplease.com/spot/civilrightstimeline1.html.

4. Dr. Martin Luther King Jr. and Clayborne Carson, *The Autobiography of Martin Luther King, Jr.* (Warner Books, 2001).

Chapter 6

1. Saint Augustine, quoted in Garry Wills, *Saint Augustine* (New York: Penguin Putnam, 1999), 139–40 and in Yancey, *Reaching for the Invisible God,* (Grand Rapids: Zondervan, 2000), 136.
2. J. I. Packer, *Knowing God,* (Downers Grove, IL: Intervarsity Press, 1973), 227.
3. Jerry Bridges, *The Pursuit of Holiness* (Colorado Springs: Navpress, 1996).

Chapter 7

1. *Christianity Today* 45, no. 12, October 1, 2001, 60.

Chapter 9

1. Piper, *Seeing and Savoring Jesus Christ,* 35–36.
2. Donald Miller, *Blue Like Jazz* (Nashville: Thomas Nelson, 2003), 131.
3. Ibid., 135.
4. Myers, *Walking with the Poor.*
5. Jim Collins, *Good to Great* (New York: HarperBusiness, 2001), 1.
6. Ibid., 10–11.

GOING DEEPER

CHAPTER 1

• Information

1. In your life, who has been the most powerful example of God's love (as Auntie Mae Mae was for me)? What are some *Truly* ways that person shaped your life? *mom, GranBert, Grace*

2. Auntie Mae Mae and Jesus were both tender in showing love and tough against injustice. How is toughness against injustice a form of love? *yern Have to Stand*

3. Read Mark 1:40–45.

   ○ What do you imagine was the sense of hope in the leper's heart as he hesitantly asked Jesus if He was willing to heal him? *Belike athes*

   ○ What do you imagine was the look on his face when Jesus reached out to touch him? *Face - who truelastiny but Pap who wite a*

   ○ How do you think the disciples might have felt at that moment? *Scared*

   ○ How did the man respond after he was cleansed?

   ○ What does this passage say to us about the potential and actual risks and rewards of touching people with God's love?

• Disturbance

4. If you were genuinely committed to defending the helpless

Signed the Unity chath. Pledge

Here I've learned to love less & look on outside more

against injustice, what actions would you take? What feelings would be produced by this commitment?

5. To what degree (low, medium, or high) do you passionately and actively care for the needs and defend the rights of "the least of these"? Explain your answer.

6. Which of the risks (facing your selfishness, not being appreciated, being ridiculed) is most threatening to you? Explain.

• *Emergence*

7. Which of the rewards for loving others (admiration, appreciation, seeing lives changed, God's smile) is most motivating to you? Explain your answer.

• *Adaptation*

8. Which of the "Lessons from Aisle 1" stood out to you? What are some ways you want to apply that lesson?

9. Why did you start reading this book? What do you hope God does in your life as you read it and apply the principles?

Again Sm grp

Engage – Look him eye

CHAPTER 2

• *Information*

1. Our genuine experience of God's grace requires two things: a heartfelt grasp of our sinfulness and of God's loving forgiveness. Both, not one or the other. Describe a time in your life when you felt very much aware of your need for forgiveness and God's grace to forgive you. *HS @ time of call*

2. Read Luke 18:9–14.

me / God

  ◦ Describe the contrast in words spoken by these two men.

  ◦ Describe the contrast in their actions. *Distone / Close*

○ If an objective observer watched your life, would he say you have the attitude of the Pharisee or of the tax collector? Explain your answer.   *Portrayed*   *Hopefully rebel*

• *Disturbance*

3. Circle the evidences of fear that you experience even occasionally:

— Feeling alone

— Feeling betrayed

Powerlessness

— Hopelessness

Worthlessness

Resentment at being controlled by others

Trying to control others

Wondering what others think of you

Shame

Guilt

No purpose

— Anxiety

Fatigue

Disproportionate anger (explosions at little things)

Apathy, or numbness

Lying

Exaggerating the truth

Irresponsibility

Overly responsible (feeling compelled to fix
    others' problems)

Loneliness

4. On a scale of 0 (not at all) to 10 (completely), how much has God's "perfect love" cast out fear (suspicion of others,

5 - Because I haven't been letting in

self-protection, etc.) in your daily experience? Be brutally honest, and explain your answer.

● *Emergence*

5. What would your life look like if you felt so secure in the love of God that you didn't react in fear or anger, and you didn't feel compelled to hide from people, dominate them, or please them to win their approval?

6. Do you agree or disagree with the statement "Seldom does God use a person greatly who has not been hurt deeply"? Explain your answer. *yes -*

● *Adaptation*

7. After reading this chapter and thinking about the need to be convicted by our own sins so that we gladly receive God's forgiveness, tell God where you are right now in this process, and invite Him to help you take the next step.

CHAPTER 3

● *Information*

1. Describe the power of physical touch. What does it mean to you to be touched by someone you trust?

2. Which of these stories of Jesus touching someone is most meaningful to you today? Explain your answer.

   ○ The Gadarene demoniac
   ○ Peter's sudden swim
   ○ Multiplying the Happy Meal
   ○ The woman who reached through people's legs
   ○ Thomas's need to touch Jesus

- *Disturbance*
  3. Think about the lines from Jack Johnson's song "The News."
     What are some reasons we don't let ourselves feel the weight
     of the pain we see on the news? How can we keep from being
     anesthetized? *Fear of Hurt & kill our us*
  4. Following is a list of different kinds of people. Indicate which
     ones you wouldn't feel completely comfortable sitting next to.
     When you've finished, look over your list and write an evalu-
     ation of your willingness to love people.

THE TOUCH TEST

*Instructions: Circle the descriptions of people you wouldn't feel comfort-
able touching and sitting next to on Sunday morning.*

A heavily tattooed man

Person with piercing through
his/her eyelids

Person who shouts
uncontrollably

Elderly single male/female

Barefoot man with a strong
body odor

Teenage male with gold teeth,
baggy pants, and cap turned
sideways

Couple living together, not
married

Interracial couple

A Muslim

Divorced female/male

Beyoncé

Non-English-speaking male/
female

New Age seeker

Extremely overweight male/
female

Couple with crying,
screaming baby

Lesbian couple

Someone with noticeable
hygiene needs

A person who sings loudly and
poorly

Someone especially quiet and meek

A Caucasian, educated, wealthy female/male

People who are married

A woman wearing pants

An articulate, well-dressed male/female

A person who talks to him-/herself (loudly)

Recovering drug addict

A Caucasian low-income male/female

Aging white male with financial resources

Woman with dirty bags of belongings

Homeless person

Man wearing baseball cap or hat

Child of middle-income parent

Teenager of middle-income parent

—Convicted sex offender

White male, not dressed in fashion

White female, not dressed in fashion

Female, more than seventy years old

Single male/female under thirty

Unemployed male/female

Person on welfare

Person who snores during service

African-American middle-class person

Illiterate adult male/female

African-American male on welfare

African-American female on welfare

Hispanic male or female

Person who answers rhetorical questions during sermon

Asian male or female

A transsexual

Arabic male or female

A convicted murderer

Mildly disabled person (needing walkers, crutches)

Disabled person

Gay male

A person who walks around during the service

Person with alcohol on breath

Person with many teeth missing

A Buddhist

Emotionally disabled person (unpredictable behavior)

Retarded youth or child

Retarded adult

Smoker	Ex-prisoner
Political conservative	Male wearing one or more
Agnostic/Atheist	earrings
Religious fanatic	Recovering sex addict
Person with dirt under finger-	Person involved in a sex scandal
nails and unkempt, dirty hair	Male, more than seventy
Female wearing tight, short skirt	years old

- **Emergence**

  5. Do you live in the inner city, the suburbs, or a rural area? Reflect on the descriptions in that section of the chapter, and identify some people around you who need your touch.

- **Adaptation**

  6. Describe the level of God's love in your spiritual tank today. Is it empty, half-full, almost full, or overflowing? Explain your answer. What would it take for it to overflow? Describe your responsibility and God's responsibility in producing the overflow; then write out your plan and pray to ask God to work powerfully in your heart.

CHAPTER 4
- **Information**

  1. After reading this chapter, what do you think it means to "see people the way Jesus saw them"? *w/ love & acceptance*
  2. Read Matthew 16:24–26.
     o What does it mean to "deny yourself"? *Ran 2nd*
     o What are some specific ways we can take up our crosses and follow Jesus?

Or Someone who don't like me

○ Read the section in the chapter about the value of each person's soul (verse 26). How does this understanding affect your thoughts about your best friend? Someone you don't like very much? A snob you know? A mentally or physically challenged person in your neighborhood?

- **Disturbance**

Always Soften

3. Would you say that God has used your pain to soften your heart and give you compassion for hurting people, or are you still in progress in this area? Explain your answer.

4. Is it intimidating or thrilling to think that loving people requires all of you? Explain your answer.

- **Emergence**

5. What are some ways "keeping score" kills love? How can you avoid keeping score so that your love won't be hindered?

Look in eyes

- **Adaptation**

6. Describe "compassion fatigue." What are some symptoms of burnout? When have you experienced these symptoms?

7. What are some specific ways you can recharge your spiritual and emotional batteries so your love for God and for people stay fresh?

Get Away & Do for Someone else

CHAPTER 5

- **Information**

1. What are some similarities and differences between holy disgust and sinful anger? (Consider motivation, triggers, volatility, goals, effects on relationships, etc.)

react, not respond

[handwritten: Getting it for Those for whom worship is a Transaction]

2. Read Matthew 10:34–39.

   ○ What are some ways the Prince of Peace intentionally causes division? *[handwritten: who Benefits]*

   ○ How does loving Jesus above everything and everyone eventually shape our responses to hurting and needy people?

   ○ Verse 39 is about counting the cost. What are some costs you'd experience if you truly followed Christ with all your heart? What would you get in return?

3. When have you recently experienced holy disgust? Describe what prompted it and how you responded.

- **Disturbance**

   4. Does it frighten you to realize that following Jesus means you will experience holy disgust as He did? Explain your answer. *[handwritten: not really]*

   5. Identify two or three examples of injustice, abuse, or abandonment in your community.

   6. Do you feel disturbed by this chapter? (I hope so.) What insight threatens or disturbs you the most?

- **Emergence**

   7. What are some factors that threaten to numb you so that you don't feel this disgust, and which keep you focused on your own desires? How can you tell when that's happening?

   8. Think about the examples of injustice, abuse, or abandonment in your world. What would it look like if you took action to defend "the least of these"?

- **Adaptation**

   9. Which of the costs of caring stand out to you? What are some costs of not caring? *[handwritten: people Lost]*

229

CHAPTER 6

- *Information*

  Eyes; Purpose

  1. Describe what it means to "have the attitude of Jesus."

  2. In what ways does it help you to realize that "God is at work in you" through the Holy Spirit? What are some evidences that the Spirit is working? What are some signs that you've blocked His work? *People Bishops*

  3. Read Luke 14:12–14. Do you agree or disagree with the statement "The measure of our commitment to Jesus is our willingness to love, give to, and serve those who cannot repay us"? Explain your answer.

- *Disturbance*

  4. All of us experience forms of resistance to loving others the way Jesus loved people. Which one described in that section of the chapter threatens to stop you (such as: excuses, a convoy mentality, fear of being misunderstood, selfish focus on wealth and comfort, desire for immediate rewards)?

  I see alot

- *Emergence*

  5. Look at the list of suggestions for taking action to touch others' lives. Go through this process right now and plan to touch three people today.

- *Adaptation*

  6. Do you know some people who are radically committed to Christ and are taking action to show His love to those who cannot repay them? If you do, how are these people affecting you at this point? How can you get more involved with them? If not, are you willing to start alone? Why or why not?

7. How would it affect your attitude and actions if you began to think of each person as Jesus? —

CHAPTER 7

• *Information*

1. Have you ever been suspicious of "preachers and church folk"? If you have, how have you voiced and acted out your suspicions?

2. In your life, who has been the best example of a spiritual leader *very* who models integrity, accountability, and God's love? How has that person changed your view of the institutional church?

3. Read John 21:15–17.

   ○ How do you think Peter felt about seeing Jesus after he betrayed Him the night before He was crucified? *Scared, Ashamed*

   ○ Why do you think Jesus asked Peter the same question three times? *So he would Hear it*

   ○ How do you think Peter felt as He responded to Jesus' questions? *Ashamed, Thug grateful*

   ○ We see Peter next in Acts as the spokesman of the early church. In what ways does a person's deep grasp of being forgiven propel him to love and serve Jesus more? *○*

• *Disturbance*

4. Can you identify with any of the descriptions of fear in that section of this chapter? How do you typically act out your fears? If *Hope / Stop Bad* you were to experience God's grace and love at the deepest place in your heart, how would it affect your fears, hopes, and dreams?

• *Emergence*

5. Some people feel very comfortable creating a different type

[handwritten left margin: Still looking?]

of church environment to make people feel welcomed, but some prefer their church's traditions. What are some things you can do to make people feel welcome even if your church culture doesn't change?

- *Adaptation*

    6. What are some specific, tangible ways you can take action to address the fears of "the least of these" outside the doors of the church in your community?

CHAPTER 8

- *Information*

    1. What does "keeping it real" mean to you? *[handwritten: Honest]*
    2. Read 2 Corinthians 11:3.
        - Paraphrase this verse. *[handwritten: I'm afraid that you'll lose focus & will withdraw]*
        - Describe what it means to be tempted to "be like God."
        - Why do you think Paul said he was "afraid" for people who would read this verse in his letter?
        - Do you think he'd be just as afraid for us today? Explain your answer. *[handwritten: yes]*
        - What do you think it means to have a "simple and pure devotion to Christ"? Is that something you're pursuing? Explain your answer.

- *Disturbance*

    3. Whether you are a pastor, staff member, or volunteer, how often do you step back and ask, "Are we becoming a rigid, life-less institution? How can we keep it fresh and real?" How would you answer those questions today?

- *Emergence*

    4. One of the new norms in this chapter is: "We demand little and expect much." What are some specific ways you can reduce the level of demands on people who come to your church? What are some ways you can communicate that you expect God to work powerfully in their lives? What difference would this norm have on your leaders, your volunteers, your members, and your visitors?   *we don't do it today*
    5. What are some forms of opposition you've experienced in your desire to show God's love to people? Describe how you plan to face those forces with strength and grace.

- *Adaptation*

    Review the "new norms" in this chapter. What is one specific norm you need to refresh or instill in your life and ministry? Write a plan for doing that, including who, what, when, where, and how. Ask God to give you grace and strength as you implement your plan.

CHAPTER 9

- *Information*

    1. Think about Jesus turning His world upside down. How closely are we following His example today? Explain your answer.
    2. In your opinion, why do so many church leaders and volunteers gravitate toward safety? Do you? What are some possible reasons?
    3. Read Acts 2:42–47.
        ◦ Describe the actions of the believers in this passage.
        ◦ Describe their relationships.

- What do you think motivated the believers to act the way they acted?
- Have you ever experienced anything like this in your life? Explain your answer.

- *Disturbance*
  4. Go back to the list of characteristics of "intentionally safe" and "intentionally spontaneous" ministries. Next to each one, rate your church or your ministry from 0 (not us at all) to 10 (yep, that's us). What does this exercise tell you about your church or organization?
  5. In what ways does being a "good" organization threaten to anesthetize against becoming "great"?

- *Emergence*
  6. Describe the impact of warmth and authenticity in a leader. And describe the impact of a leader who lacks these qualities.
  7. What are some reasons people wear masks and play roles? What can we expect from ourselves, from God, and from others as we become more transparent and trustworthy?

- *Adaptation*
  8. After reading this chapter, what is the first (or next) step in your becoming "intentionally different" by living a life of authenticity before God?

CHAPTER 10
- *Information*
  1. How would you describe the risks and rewards of serving Jesus?

2. Read Revelation 1:12–18.

- ○ Try to describe the image of Jesus John experienced that day.
- ○ When was a time when you felt "blown away" by the greatness of Jesus?
- ○ How would it affect your motivation if you reflected often on John's vision of Jesus?

- *Disturbance*

   3. What difference does it make to live "in the moment" instead of living in the successes or failures of the past or in the worries of the future? To what extent do you live "in the moment"? What do you need to do to live "in the moment" more than you do right now?

   4. What are some differences between ministering as a right and ministering as a privilege? Which one characterizes your life right now? Explain your answer.

- *Emergence*

   5. As you reflect on what you've read in this book, what is the most important thing you've learned?

   6. How will you make this a vital and consistent part of your life?

- *Adaptation*

   7. What is your next step in soaking up the love of God so His love will overflow into the lives of those in your community?

   8. What are some ways you can help others in your church grasp these principles, sense the disturbance they cause in us, and take action to create movements of God to touch the lives of every person in your community—from the wealthy to "the least of these"?

ABOUT THE AUTHOR

Rudy Rasmus is an urban messenger and co-pastor with his wife, Juanita, of St. John's United Methodist Church, located in Downtown Houston.

Beginning with nine existing members in 1992, St. John's has grown to more than 9,000 members—3,000 either are, or formerly were, homeless. The church is one of the most culturally diverse congregations in the country. Every week people of every social and economic background share the same pew. Pastor Rudy attributes the success of the church to a compassionate congregation that has embraced the vision of tearing down the walls of classism, sexism, and racism and building bridges of unconditional love. The church is known for its infectious hope that God will change lives.

To meet the physical needs of the community, Pastor Rudy cofounded Bread of Life, Inc. (a not-for-profit corporation) in December of 1992 and began serving dinners to the homeless in the sanctuary at St. John's. Today, Bread of Life has become a lighthouse of love, providing an array of services to homeless men and women seven days a week in the recently constructed Daybreak Community Health Facility on the St. John's campus. Bread of Life currently provides more than 7,000 hot meals and 80,000 pounds of fresh food each month to hungry and homeless individuals. On a daily basis, the agency also provides health and dental care for the indigent and uninsured, job training and placement, substance abuse and psychiatric counseling, and HIV testing, prevention, and education.

In 1999, Pastor Rudy also cofounded St. John's Academy to provide a safe and stable environment for the children of this community, especially those living with HIV-AIDS, exposure to drugs and alcohol, and other developmental delays.

Over the past five years, campus construction has totaled $5 million, including state-of-the-art renovations to the Center for Worship and the construction of the Center for Hope. Thanks to a generous donation from Kelly Rowland and Beyoncé Knowles of the pop singing group Destiny's Child, the campus includes the $1.2 million Knowles-Rowland Center for Youth, an exciting, multipurpose recreational complex for young people in the community.

In the aftermath of Hurricane Katrina in 2005, St. John's began construction of the Temenos Place Apartments. This project will include a 50-unit single room occupancy development designed to provide transitional living accommodations for women and men who are taking significant steps to improve their lives.

Pastors Rudy and Juanita have been married for twenty-one years and are the proud parents of two daughters, Morgan and Ryan.

HOW TO BEGIN
A MINISTRY TO
HOMELESS PEOPLE

When Jesus walked on earth, He taught about the kingdom while He healed the sick, restored sight to the blind, and fed the hungry. Today, we are called to meet the physical as well as the spiritual needs of people—*all* the people—in our communities. In fact, hurting and hungry people won't believe we care if they only hear our words but don't see our actions to provide tangible help for them.

Many of us drive by hurting, hungry, and homeless people every day without giving them a second thought, but when God touches our hearts and motivates us to care for "the least of these," we want to get involved—in fact, we *have to* get involved because we have a sense of urgency to help them. But we shouldn't rush into this ministry. We need to do our homework, clarify our goals, and find good resources so that our efforts will be successful.

To have a strong, vibrant ministry to the homeless, incorporate these five "Cs":

- *Common Sense*
  The streets are a tough place with real risks. Many street people

are courteous and kind, but some are addicts who consider robbing people because they desperately need money for their next hit; some are unstable because they suffer from chronic mental illness; and some are hiding from the police or parole officers because they have broken the law. Be aware of your surroundings and go in teams, with a good blend of men and women to be sure women aren't unnecessarily vulnerable. Early in our work with homeless people around St. John's, some of our volunteers were robbed, so we hired security guards for our homeless ministry.

• Collaboration

Local government and non-profit agencies offer a wide variety of resources for hungry and homeless people, such as mental health services, clothing, food, and legal assistance. Discover the help that's available, and team with agencies that can assist your efforts. These agencies have been providing assistance to the disadvantaged in your community for years. Enlist them to train your volunteers, and ask for their advice as you clarify your strategy for your ministry.

• Commitment

People on the street may look like they don't have a clue, but they can tell if people who come to help them genuinely care, or if they are just on a one-time, social experiment to earn a merit badge. For this reason, be sure that the leadership of the church "own" this ministry and give plenty of emotional, spiritual, and tangible support to those who are helping the homeless. Blending spiritual care with physical assistance is a powerful ministry, but most homeless people trust others very reluctantly. It will take time and tenacity to earn their trust.

• *Consistency*

Look for people, agencies, and corporate partners who will join you for the long haul in this ministry. People on the street need to see familiar faces on a regular basis so they can believe that you truly care about them. As they see you and your team as consistent and reliable, you'll earn their respect. At that point, they might listen to your message of hope and forgiveness, and they might take steps based on your loving advice.

• *Contributions*

Donations to this ministry come in all shapes, in all sizes, and from all sources. Our church's confirmation classes collect socks and warm caps each winter to give to homeless people. Others give toys, clothes, blankets, and money to meet needs of street people. St. John's has a corporate partner whose employees give their time one day each month to feed the homeless. Look for additional sources of help from other non-profits and businesses in your community. When people realize how much homeless people need help, their hearts are broken and they open the doors of their resources to assist them. Make the need known, and ask people to be generous.

Beginning and developing a ministry to people on the street is rewarding, but it can also be exhausting. Set clear goals and establish a workable strategy. Ask plenty of questions, build a great team, and look for resources to help you. If your heart is broken because you see the needs of men, women, boys, and girls on the street, enlist the leaders of your church to pray and help you communicate God's love in a tangible way to those who desperately need it. As God leads you to build your team and find resources, take action to touch the lives of "the least of these." It will be one of the most fulfilling things you've ever done.

241

HOW TO LEAD A TOUCH GROUP OR CLASS

This book is designed for individual study, small groups, and classes. The best way to absorb and apply these principles is for each person to individually study and answer the questions at the end of the chapters, then to discuss them in either a class or a group environment.

The questions and exercises are designed to promote reflection, application, and discussion. Order enough copies of the book for each person to have their own. For couples, encourage both to have their own book so they can record their individual thoughts and prayers.

A recommended schedule for a small group might be:

Week 1   Introduction to the material. The group leader can tell their own story, share their hopes for the group, and provide books for each person.

Weeks 2–11   Cover chapters 1–10, one chapter per week.

Week 12   Discuss the way God has worked in your lives, your plans to apply the principles in your families and friendships, and the ways you can help your church touch your community.

PERSONALIZE EACH LESSON

Make sure you personalize the principles and applications. At least once in each group meeting, add your own story to illustrate a particular point.

Make the Scriptures come alive. Far too often, we read the Scriptures like it's a phone book, with little or no emotion. Paint a vivid picture for people. Provide insights about the context of the encounters with Jesus, and help people sense the emotions of specific people in each scene.

FOCUS ON APPLICATION

The questions at the end of the chapters and the encouragement to be authentic will help your group "get real" about the touch of Jesus. Share how you are applying the principles in the chapter, and encourage them to take steps of growth, too.

THREE TYPES OF QUESTIONS

If you have led groups for few years, you already understand the importance of using open questions to stimulate discussion. Three types of questions are *limiting, leading,* and *open.*

- *Limiting questions* focus on an obvious answer, such as, "What does Jesus call himself in John 10:11?" These don't stimulate reflection or discussion. If you want to use questions like this, follow them with thought-provoking open questions.

- *Leading questions* sometimes require the listener to guess what the leader has in mind, such as, "Why did Jesus use the metaphor of a shepherd in John 10?" (He was probably alluding to a passage in Ezekiel, but most people wouldn't know that.) The teacher who asks a leading question has a definite answer in mind. Instead of asking this question, he should teach the point and perhaps ask an open question about the point he has made.

○ *Open questions* usually don't have right or wrong answers. They stimulate thinking, and they are far less threatening because the person answering doesn't risk ridicule for being wrong. These questions often begin with "Why do you think . . . ?" or "What are some possible reasons that . . . ?" or "How would you have felt in that situation?"

PREPARATION

As you prepare to teach this material in a group, consider these steps:

1. Carefully and thoughtfully read the book. Make notes, highlight key sections, quotes, or stories, and complete the reflection sections at the end of each chapter. This will familiarize you with the entire scope of the content.

2. As you prepare for each lesson, read the corresponding chapter again and make additional notes.

3. Tailor the amount of content to the time allotted. You may not have time to cover all the questions, so pick the ones that are most pertinent.

4. Add your own stories to personalize the message and add impact.

5. Before and during your preparation, ask God to give you wisdom, clarity, and power. Trust Him to use your group to change people's lives.

6. Most people will get far more out of the group if they read the book each week. Order books before the class begins or after the first week.